CRICKET WORLD CUP '83

One word could have been used to describe the approach to the third Prudential World Cup competition: disarray. It was true of the great powers and added spice to the hopes of the secondary nations. There were few of the certainties of 1975 or 1979 and all through one of England's dampest springs, as the cricketers flew into Heathrow, the bronzed and the black, they could all see the rainbow.

True, the champions West Indies had continued to win but, Marshall apart, the great fast-bowling machine was more than thirty years old. Lloyd and Richards were as charismatic as ever but it was eight years since that first great and glorious final at Lord's.

True, Australia had won the World Series Cup in Sydney the previous winter, yet they had approached those finals as third favourites behind England and New Zealand. Leadership and consistency were almost as important as talent.

When the selectors met to choose England's squad, cynics suggested that Willis and Gower were the only two certainties and Willis only because he was the captain. Pakistan were worried about the fitness of their new emperor, Imran Khan, while India had been shattered by successive Test defeats by Pakistan and West Indies.

There was far less depression elsewhere. New Zealand smiled in practice, the Sri Lankans were as ever irrepressibly cheerful and Zimbabwe always appeared conscious that they had more to prove than their cricketing ability.

The contributors

Dickie Rutnagur (**DR**) is not, as Peter Tinniswood avers, a maharajah, although head waiters believe him to be. He writes cricket, squash and badminton for the *Daily Telegraph* and reported India's recent Caribbean campaign.

David Lemmon (**DL**) is the editor of *Benson and Hedges Cricket Year* and the author of a delightful biography of 'Tich' Freeman. His latest work is the *Wisden Book of Cricket Quotations*. Graham Otway (**GO**), as the Press Association's Cricket Correspondent, reported England in India and Australia while his colleague, Ray Dye (**RD**), covering Ian Botham's stormy England tour of West Indies, was often heard to sigh for the cold rain and warm bitter of Blackheath.

Jack Bannister (**JB**), 1500 wickets for Warwickshire under his belt, is now Cricket Correspondent of the *Birmingham Post* and has a keen eye at the service of the punter. On dull days in the Midlands the chief cricket writer for the Raymond's Agency, Neil Hallam (**NH**), changes the Derbyshire captaincy.

Mike Beddow (**MB**) is a leading Midlands soccer and cricket writer and lives near Stratford, modestly disowning comparisons with another local writer, while Pat Symes (**PS**) decorates Hampshire and the South with his phrases and was co-author, with Gordon Greenidge, of *Man in the Middle*.

The hope of everyone connected with this report is that their enjoyment of this magnificent tournament is communicated to you.

DEREK HODGSON

World Cup cricket – the story so far . . .

I f Prudential, Heaven forbid, should ever become another South Sea Bubble and collapse in a sea of debts, they would still be remembered fondly 100 years from today. Their support, encouragement and increasingly substantial backing of three World Cup competitions has given cricket its greatest spectacle, a one-day tournament that has been so successful that it has earned hardly a word of criticism and won the admiration of the crustiest traditionalists.

They were lucky to choose a summer to start with, in 1975, that must have been lifted from the Edwardian Golden Age. Fifteen 60-over matches were played from 7 June to 21 June in brilliant weather. Day after day the sun shone with such a fierce consistency that even Manchester and Swansea were soon crying of drought.

The super-powers were West Indies and Australia. Ian Chappell's team boasted Lillee and Thomson, the opening attack that had blasted Mike Denness's England side to rubble in Australia the previous winter. Clive Lloyd's West Indians were still climbing to their peak but the prospect of watching the stroke-play promised by their batting order – Greenidge, Kanhai, Kallicharran, Lloyd and the young Richards – must have made many a youngster of whatever nationality too excited to eat breakfast.

No-one seriously expected a real challenge to this pair from a shell-shocked England under Tony Greig, from a Pakistan lightweight in seam bowling, or from the grave, ascetic Indians, who all too often seemed to regard limited-overs play as a conversation in Mongolian.

1975 – the group matches

The draw favoured England, who promptly romped through their group with substantial victories over India, New Zealand and East Africa, Amiss being the outstanding contributor.

Australia began at Headingley, against Pakistan, and for the first time in nine years the gates were closed before the start with 22,000 inside. Pakistan, needing 279, threatened a surprising victory when they were 172 for 4 with 20 overs left. Lillee's dismissal of Asif, one of five victims for 34 runs, was the turning point.

Patrick Eagar

Alvin Kallicharran hooks Dennis Lillee for another boundary during his stunning innings in the group match at the Oval in 1975.

Patrick Eagar

Clive Lloyd in aggressive mood during his match-winning innings in the 1975 final.

One of three amazing run-outs in which Viv Richards was involved during the Australian innings at Lord's in 1975. This time the victim is Alan Turner.

New Zealand, and not Pakistan, were the unexpected semi-finalists, and were unable to match West Indian power at the Oval. At Leeds, 18 June 1975 will be remembered as Gilmour's Day. On a green pitch and under a cloudy sky, Australia's fast-medium left-hander was able to swing the ball and seam it off the pitch, finishing with 6 for 14 as England were shattered, all out for 93 in less than 37 overs.

Nor had Gilmour finished. When England's bowlers reduced Australia to 39 for 6, he and Walters fashioned victory with an unbroken stand of 55. The final was no less

Encouraged, Pakistan went to Birmingham to put West Indies through an unexpected fire in a magnificent match that went to the fourth ball of the last over, West Indies getting home by one wicket. The clash of the titans came at the Oval on 14 June, where Lloyd sent Australia in on a cloudy morning and Boyce disposed of both the Chappells within six balls. Marsh was left 52 not out in a disappointing total of 192 with six overs left unused.

Kallicharran's assault on Lillee will be long remembered. In an innings of 78 he hit a six and 13 fours, hooking and driving superbly, taking 35 off the last ten balls he received from the great Australian. Brixton has never been quite the same.

The ball is soaring over the long leg boundary, but Roy Fredericks slips and is out, hit wicket, to Lillee.

anticipated because it was expected: Australia v West Indies at Lord's.

The 1975 final

And what a final! It began at 11 am and ended at 8.43. There may never be a better one-day match. From the moment Roy Fredericks trod on his wicket, after hooking a bouncer for six, to the last, defiant bat-swinging of Lillee and Thomson, the final salvoes of a sinking battleship, the match had a 26,000 crowd enthralled.

At one point West Indies were 50 for 3, with Greenidge spending 80 minutes over 13, but once Lloyd arrived, to play one of his many

HRH Prince Philip watches Clive Lloyd hold up the first Prudential Cup.

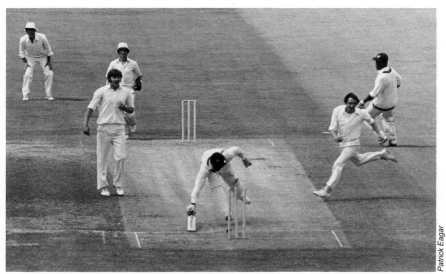

Patrick Eagar

'Arkle' strikes again: Gordon Greenidge fails to beat Derek Randall's throw in the 1979 final.

great innings, the final swung inexorably towards the Caribbean. He hooked Lillee square for six and went on to add another six and 12 fours, 102 runs in 108 minutes. With Kanhai he raised the score by 149 in 36 overs. Asked today if it was his greatest innings, Clive smiles and says, 'It was certainly among the most enjoyable'.

Australia needed 292, which meant a long, controlled haul at a steadily increasing tempo. The tensions made them erratic, their running between wickets disintegrated and brilliant West Indian fielding brought five run-outs, among them the Chappells who were, according to Clive Lloyd (sounding like the town marshal of St John's Wood), 'as dangerous as the James brothers in the old Wild West'.

Nevertheless the final margin was only 17 runs, tight enough to keep everyone in suspense till late on a golden evening. The Duke of Edinburgh presented the Prudential Cup, the takings totalled £200,000 and the only flaw in an otherwise perfect competition was the absence of South Africa.

The preliminaries, 1979

Looking backwards from 1979, the year of the second World Cup, to 1975 must be for a cricketer rather like seeing 1913 from 1917. The intervening years were disputatious and controversial as Test players, encouraged and supported by the Australian magnate, Kerry Packer, sought to bring their earnings into line with golf and tennis professionals. The ethics of the argument are immaterial to the impact it had on world cricket and Australia, certainly, were still trying to come to terms with the divisions when the Cup tournament opened.

West Indies, in contrast, were even stronger. Clive Lloyd had a fast attack unequalled in history and their likely final opponents this time were England, a weaker team but so astutely led by Brearley.

The weather, too, was mixed. The

Patrick Eagar

Danger-man Kallicharran is bowled by Hendrick for 4 – Lord's, 1979.

The power of Collis King during the 1979 final.

Bob Taylor can only watch and admire as Viv Richards dismisses the ball from his presence during his Man-of-the-Match 138.

Patrick Eagar

The enthusiastic crowd watches Clive Lloyd receive the Prudential Cup for a second time.

Patrick Eagar

and Willis had added 43. A spell of four wickets in eight balls for three runs by Hendrick – followed by a dazzling catch – blotted out Pakistan's stars, but their highly capable tail was functioning well until Boycott, to the huge delight of Headingley, tempted out the last two batsmen and England won by 14 runs.

There was another shock for England at Old Trafford, where New Zealand's big hitters failed by only nine runs to overtake a total of 221. West Indies, running up 293 for 6, left Pakistan comfortably behind at the Oval.

West Indies again

The final question became: could the wily Brearley outpoint the big-punching Lloyd? England gambled by preferring an extra batsman which meant, with Willis injured, they had only four specialist bowlers.

Sent in, West Indies lost their first four wickets for 99 as England bowled tightly and fielded brilliantly, Randall especially. Then came a devastating innings of 138 by Richards while King savaged England's batsmen-bowlers, Boycott, Gooch and Larkins.

Yet if West Indies thought the match won, they had to wait while Boycott and Brearley raised 129, leaving England to get 158 off the final 22 overs. A slightly faster rate by the opening pair would have helped (Richards was allowed to bowl ten overs for 35) before the 6′8″ Garner, bowling with the Nursery End trees behind him and in fading light, ripped through the order, taking five wickets for four runs in 11 balls.

So Lloyd took the cup again, this time by a margin of 92 runs; Lord's resembled a carnival day in Port of Spain. Another all-ticket crowd of 25,000 streamed away and over the beer or wine that evening the conversation was already turning to the third World Cup in 1983.

three Saturdays stayed fine but rain intervened to wash out the West Indies v Sri Lanka match at the Oval and England lost the first day of their Old Trafford match against Canada.

Pakistan were the danger although again, they hadn't the seam bowling to match their superb batting array. They did give England a terrible fright at Leeds, sending them in, reducing them to 118 for 8 and finally needing only 166 to win after Taylor

Rain decides – the mixture as before

Whatever plans and ideas the England's selectors may have had in mind to rebuild the team that lost the Ashes and the World Series Cup in Australia (and was then trounced by New Zealand) had to be postponed temporarily.

After one of the wettest springs in history there was just not enough evidence to make wholesale changes. No young player outside the immediate circle of candidates had been allowed the opportunity to impress himself upon selectorial vision. No-one could admit it, but in the end the England squad was selected on the principle of 'the devil you know'.

Appointment of captain

An indication of the way of the wind came with the early re-appointment of Bob Willis as captain for the World Cup. In the past, England captains with more successful campaigns than Willis had disappeared without trace, but there seemed little point in changing a leader respected by his team if that team were to be left virtually unchanged.

So the hard core of the winter campaigners were chosen again: Graeme Fowler was clearly the most successful opening batsman in England, while Chris Tavare had managed both to make runs and to captain Kent successfully.

The real debate

David Gower was now accepted as England's number one batsman. Allan Lamb, too, kept his place as a potential world-class batsman. Derek Randall deserved to stay both as batsman and as fielder. Ian Botham could not be omitted so the real debate must have centred upon Willis's seam partners, the name of the spinner and that of the wicket-keeper.

Universal praise

Four more survivors from Australia were called to fight again: Norman Cowans as the fastest bowler, Ian Gould as the wicket-keeper, Trevor Jesty as the reserve all-rounder (although he had done very little bowling) and Vic Marks as the off-spinner, to counter Australia's army of left-handers.

The three newcomers to make up the 14 won universal praise although, in fact, all had played for England in Test matches. Graham Dilley, the outstanding English fast-bowling prospect of the last five years, had wintered well in South Africa.

Bowling accurately

Paul Allott, the tall Lancastrian, was bowling accurately again after a disappointing 1982 in which he had carried a pelvic strain. Mike Gatting, ignored during the winter, had re-emerged as Middlesex captain with apparently no diminution in his appetite for runs. Gatting's combative batting and aggressive close fielding made him invaluable for this cricket and there were hints that his bowling might be useful.

What might have been

Traditionalists would have preferred another spinner, especially as the squad seemed to contain at least one spare batsman.

What the squad needed was another bowler who could bat but, sadly, the two outstanding candidates, John Emburey and Arnie Sidebottom, were 'disqualified' players because of their South African connections. Once again, the highly talented and versatile Phil Edmonds was ignored.

Adrian Murrell/All-Sport

David Gower was England's one bright shining star in Australia last winter, even winning praise from that ferocious critic of contemporary players, F. S. Trueman: 'David is blossoming into a great batsman.'

Too many left-handers for comfort?

Australia landed with a spotted escutcheon. Winners of the World Series Cup last winter in Australia, when the critics were choosing England and New Zealand for the final, they then toured Sri Lanka and lost two full international one-day games to the world's newest Test nation.

There were, of course, differences between the World Series winners and the tourists up in delightful Kandy (no Lawson, for one) and Australia did go on to win the only Test match of the tour by the crushing margin of an innings and 38 with a day to spare. Yet the suspicion that modern Australian teams are no longer conspicuously successful tourists remained, as did the feeling that assimilation, in such a short term as the World Cup provides, would be a problem for Kim Hughes and his manager, Phil Ridings.

Surprise

The Australian selectors surprised recent opponents by their omission of that gritty all-rounder, Bruce Yardley, preferring the youngest of the Chappells, Trevor, now 30, for the role of, to use an Irishism, the specialist bits-and-pieces player.

The seam attack looked formidable even without the sad absence of Terry Alderman, still recovering from the shoulder injury sustained in Perth. A captain who can select from Lillee, Lawson, Thomson and Hogg is rich but Hughes must have spent many a quiet moment on the way over working on his permutations.

Five specialist bowlers are needed and the good sides carry a back-up bowler. Hughes had Chappell and he could also call on the West Australian slow left-hander, Tom Hogan, but those and the four quickies, apart from the slow rollers of Allan Border, represented his entire bowling strength.

Hughes also had to accept that on England's softer surfaces and in heavier air, conditions that might

Adrian Murrell/All-Sport

Geoff Lawson is now Australia's strike bowler, a lean, whippy New South Welshman who has learned much in the last two years in the company of Lillee and Thomson. 'Too nice a guy to be an Aussie fast bowler,' say England's batsmen. Such compliments haven't seduced 'Henry' into abandoning his fearsome bouncer.

suit Lillee and perhaps Lawson and Hogg, would be foreign to Jeff Thomson, who needs pace and bounce in the pitch. Neither Thomson nor Hogg had been successful in England and the conclusion had to be, back in early June, that Alderman had left a gap that could not be filled.

Solid batting

The withdrawal of Greg Chappell, with a neck injury sustained against England last December, a problem that has hampered his bowling since, meant the loss of not only Australia's most distinguished batsman but also the absence of a useful relief bowler. His replacement, the 23-year-old Western Australia all-rounder, Ken MacLeay, had forced his way into the Australian team for the World Series finals after an outstanding season for his State both in the Sheffield Shield and in one-day matches.

Even without Greg Chappell, the batting looked solid. Wessels, once a prolific scorer with Sussex, was already English-oriented. Wood, seasoned and able, hoped to have put his 'Kamikaze Kid' days behind him and any levity he may have felt in stealing runs was always liable to be quashed by his stern partner.

Two powerful left-handers of different styles, Yallop and Hookes were to follow with Hughes himself, a distinguished and popular batsman in England.

Questions to be answered

No batsman stood higher in English eyes than Border, now firmly embedded in history as one of the great last-ditchers while the ebullient Marsh returned yet again, seemingly indestructible. But every time the Australians appeared the questions flowed: was Lillee still that dark angel of destruction? Was Thommo just a wheezing old engine in English damps and dews? And how would Australia's left-handers fare against the ritual off-spin of England?

Cracks might show, but still great

Six fast bowlers spearheaded the West Indies' attempt to hold on to the World Cup they won in 1975 and 1979. Six – and they were unable to choose Colin Croft, Franklyn Stephenson or Ezra Moseley, all of whom had played in South Africa!

Yet the perceptive 'Windies-watchers' were saying that the selection was in fact an attempt to camouflage weakness rather than a boastful display of strength. Of the six, Andy Roberts and Joel Garner were both over 30 while the superb Michael Holding was in his thirtieth year.

The long-discarded Wayne Daniel was recalled from Middlesex, at 27, while Winston Davis of Glamorgan, 24, was relatively inexperienced. Malcolm Marshall of Hampshire, however, was the chief wicket-taker in England in 1982 and has become a world-class bowler.

Doubts

West Indies had chosen six, it was suggested, because they were uncertain how many of their noble old guard would last the course. Two batsmen, Viv Richards and Larry Gomes, would provide gentle off-spin if ever it was needed.

There were also doubts about the batting and captain Clive Lloyd admitted, before the competition began, that he needed his youngsters to succeed.

Gordon Greenidge and Desmond Haynes are, certainly in one-day matches, the world's best opening pair. Two fluent, hard-hitting Bajans, scarred veterans of World Series cricket, there is very little left in cricket to surprise them. Even the deputy opener, Faoud Bacchus, is a highly experienced tourist and a former Young West Indies captain.

World's number one

Viv Richards remains, by unanimous judgement of his peers, the world's number one batsman. Opposing captains are grateful that he remains a basically happy-go-lucky Antiguan – with a dash of Somerset – and does not possess the temperament of a Bradman or a Boycott.

Geniality and goodwill

Clive Lloyd's greatest gift to cricket, apart from being one of the most spectacular entertainers in history, has been his ability to reign over the fastest attack, one that has spread terror everywhere, with such geniality and goodwill that the world championship was won and held with virtually no acrimony and good-will on every side. As they say in Manchester, 'That Clive's a lovely lad'.

Jeff Dujon is the new wicket-keeper, Gomes is a batsman of such class that Middlesex must regret releasing him, while Gus Logie is a right-handed version of Alvin Kallicharran.

Fascinating and brilliant

A fascinating side, brilliant in so many facets, yet carrying a suspicion of brittleness about them. The World Cup, like any one-day tournament, demanded fielding of the highest standard and for that a team needs hungry young men. Did West Indies have enough of those? Were there too many field marshals, heavy with honours and medals, in the side?

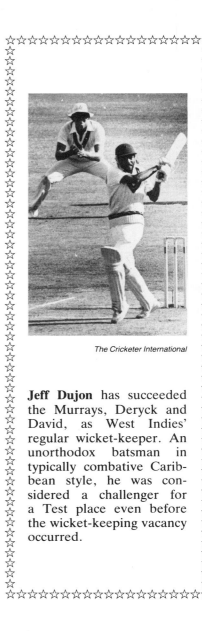

The Cricketer International

Jeff Dujon has succeeded the Murrays, Deryck and David, as West Indies' regular wicket-keeper. An unorthodox batsman in typically combative Caribbean style, he was considered a challenger for a Test place even before the wicket-keeping vacancy occurred.

Dark horses with ability and experience

Any heated confrontation between the captains of England and New Zealand could always be resolved by a line from Bob Dylan. Geoff Howarth didn't go as far as R. G. Willis and add 'Dylan' to his forenames, but he shares an admiration for the singer-poet.

Howarth, 32, led a side whose prestige in one-day circles had rocketed. From no-hopers they became everyone's favourite dark horse; at long last, it seemed, New Zealand was learning how to use every inch of ability in the most effective manner.

Measured temperament

The Crowe brothers are a good example. Sons of a first-class player, Jeff, still only 24, spent six seasons playing Sheffield Shield cricket with South Australia. Martin, 20, like his brother a right-handed bat, was a powerful player of great hitting potential, over 6ft and 14 stone.

Another is Martin Snedden, much favoured as a future Test captain. A 24-year-old solicitor, he bats left-handed and bowls right, and allies a cool and measured temperament to a good eye and natural ability.

Hadlee the match-winner

John Wright's advent should have warned us of New Zealand's grow-ing power. His left-hand batting for Derbyshire prompted John Hamp-shire to rate him among the world's best openers. With Glenn Turner, who *is* one of the world's best openers and the most prolific scorer in New Zealand's history, the Kiwis began with the oldest-established and most experienced opening part-nership in the tournament.

There are those who would argue that Martin Donnelly and Bert Sutcliffe come before Turner as New Zealand's best. No one argues about Richard Hadlee, who lines up along-side Botham, Imran Khan and Clive Rice among the world's greatest all-rounders. A match-winning fast bowler at the highest level, his fast bowling developed not by strength but through an immaculate, finely tuned action from a lean and whippy frame, Hadlee also became, in his magnificent service to Notts, a ferocious punisher of loose and sometimes good bowling.

Bruce Edgar is the rock-solid left-hander every team needs, a player of sound technique and stubborn temperament who would surely have done as well as Wright had he entered English county cricket.

Warren Lees, 31 and 17 Tests, is the wicket-keeper batsman all captains seek. Apart from one Test century and appearances as high as no. 6 in the order, he is also good enough with the gloves to leave no-one in doubt as to why he was in the team. Ewen Chatfield is as experi-enced and steady a quick bowler as any in international cricket.

Prodigious hitting

Jeremy Coney's close-wicket catch-ing was described by Robin Marlar as 'adhesive'. He is the dressing room's funny-man but arrived in England only a few short of 1,000 runs in Tests. Opposing bowlers do not laugh often.

Lance Cairns's prodigious hitting powers have frightened the oppo-sition world-wide. On the last tour he amazed audiences at Old Trafford and Scarborough. He is especially feared in the one-day

Adrian Murrell/All-Sport

Geoff Howarth, highly re-garded by his peers as a player, has recently won much public attention in New Zealand and abroad for his captaincy. Under Howarth, the Kiwis have become a well-trained and tactically astute one-day team.

game because of his power to turn the match in 12 balls. As a bowler he maintains a lively, accurate attack for hours.

John Bracewell, an off-spinner, is the older brother of the highly promising fast bowler, Brendon Bracewell, who so sadly lost form after the 1978 tour. Ian Smith arrived as Warren Lees's deputy but had already won seven caps.

9

Optimistic and intriguing, and no pushover

Kapil Dev never seems to stop smiling and a cheerful optimism would appear to be a vital element in any captain of India. The post, carrying with it an internal and international prestige that rivals only that of the Prime Minister, is surrounded with so much intrigue and back-stabbing that some occupants would have felt safer in the company of Cesare Borgia.

Increasing tactical awareness

'Laugh and the world laughs with you' seemed to be Kapil's motto in leading a World Cup team constructed from a Test side that has just lost to Pakistan and West Indies and whom were well beaten by England on their last visit here. That doesn't mean India could be regarded as a pushover at one-day cricket.

Their increasing tactical awareness was very evident to an England team captained by the astute Keith Fletcher in Jullundur and Cuttack on the last tour. Apart from Dev himself, a match-winner of Botham-like proportions on his day, India developed other players capable of the sudden volcanic efforts that decide these fixtures.

Sunil Gavaskar, for instance, possesses more than the tenacity of a Boycott. He straight-drove John Lever for six in the opening overs of the Jubilee Test in Bombay and his demolition of Yorkshire a year ago is still remembered. He can score quickly, as can India's most successful one-day batsman, Yashpal Sharma, their elegant no. 3, Dilip Vengsarkar, and the singing film star, Sandeep Patil.

Affection and respect

India arrived with a new vice-captain, Mohinder Amarnath, a very experienced all-rounder in a side that tried to compensate for its weakness in seam-bowling with an array of bowlers who could bat like Kirti Azad (medium-pace off-cutters), Roger Binny, and the veteran quick bowler, Madan Lal.

The wicket-keeper was, of course, Syed Kirmani, known as 'Kojak' for obvious reasons to the England dressing room, a nickname that might have been of little significance in Kanpur but indicates the affection and respect of his opponents.

Ravi Shastri had added a West Indian tour to his packed 21 years, another seasoning of experience to a gifted young man of enormous versatility. The player many looked forward to watching in England was the controversial opening batsman, Kris Srikkanth.

A functioning anarchy

A right-hander who has always believed the ball was bowled to be hit, Srikkanth's innings tend to be brief but very explosive while they last. A modicum of luck in the first two overs and Srikkanth is able to score so fast that opposing captains, seeing the new ball hurtling round the fences, despair of getting back into the game.

Sunil Valson is a left-arm medium-pace bowler whose selection was the one major surprise in the party. Balwinder Singh has played in seven Tests and is a lively swing bowler with the new ball, has scored a 71 against Pakistan and can claim what must be a unique performance: he bowled both Greenidge and Haynes for ducks in Port of Spain.

India has been described as a functioning anarchy and Kapil's team reflected national characteristics: not always successful, sometimes placid, delightfully sociable, intriguing competitors and fascinating opponents, a team and a country for students and lovers (of cricket, of course).

Adrian Murrell/All-Sport

Ravi Shastri is still only 20 and is on his third trip to England (once as a school-boy, once as a 1982 tourist). A tall, talented, slow left-arm bowler, he has needed his batting ability to maintain a place, squeezed between the experienced Dilip Doshi and the new star, Maninder Singh.

A team of talented individuals

Pakistan left a glittering impression on their short 1982 tour of England, a panoply of power worthy of the durbar of a Moghul Emperor. They and West Indies were the two teams in the World Cup acknowledged to be capable of winning from the start: the abiding question with Pakistan was whether they could concentrate and sustain their abilities.

Imran Khan, their captain, epitomised their difficulties. He was unable to play for his county, Sussex, because of a stress fracture of his right shin and had already told the selectors he had no wish to be considered for the later tour of India. Any diminution of the power of the world's fastest bowler and, on the form of 1982, the world's leading all-rounder, had to weaken the overall strength of the side and dent morale.

Unfamiliar and untried

With the other opening bowler, Sarfraz Nawaz, approaching the day of retirement, the Pakistani seam attack smacked of the unfamiliar and the untried. Tahir Naqquash had impressed English batsmen with his strength, increasing pace and ability to move the ball either way in his limited opportunities on the 1982 tour.

Two more medium-to-fast seamers were included, Rashid Khan, who took 55 wickets in domestic cricket and had the reputation of being a useful batsman, and Shahid Mahboob, another all-rounder who, at 20 years of age, was reputed to be developing pace. Shahid also arrived with the invaluable experience of 89 wickets for the Bradford League club Hartshead Moor.

Abdul Qadir

One name branded on English memories was that of Abdul Qadir, whose dazzling leg-spin and googly

bowling lifted the 1982 season and left English critics enraptured. He was less popular with the English batsmen who had to deal with him. The Australians were even more impressed: he took 22 Test wickets on their last tour of Pakistan.

That aggressive all-rounder, Wasim Raja, recently lost his place in the Test side but it seemed unlikely that such a fierce competitor, whose leg-breaks and googlies add another weapon to the attack, would be omitted from the World Cup side.

Wasim Bari is now as permanent a feature of Pakistan as the Khyber Pass, the difference being that this brilliant wicket-keeper batsman (73 Tests) allows little to go through.

Batting strength

The jewels in the crown were the batsmen. Mohsin Khan and Mudassar Nazar, 57 Tests between them, are an experienced and reliable pair of openers talented enough to regulate the tempo of any innings against any bowling. There followed the bespectacled Zaheer Abbas, one of the world's best with 11 Test centuries, four of them double-hundreds. For Gloucestershire he has four times scored a double-century and a century in the same match and at 36 has passed the 100 centuries.

Javed Miandad has flayed most bowling around the world. At 26 he has already hit ten Test centuries including two double-hundreds. Mansoor Akhtar, 25, scored 224 not out when he became joint holder (with Waheed Mirza) of the world's highest opening stand, 561, in the 1976–7 season.

Ejaz Fakih, 27, is a right-handed all-rounder who bowls off-breaks and who has won a reputation as a useful performer in one-day games, a good enough player to keep up pressure on the stars.

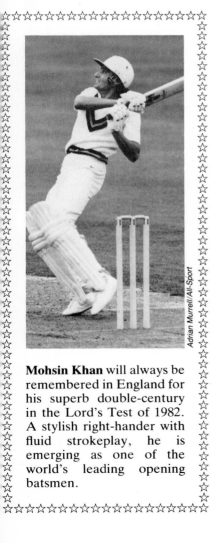

Adrian Murrell/All-Sport

Mohsin Khan will always be remembered in England for his superb double-century in the Lord's Test of 1982. A stylish right-hander with fluid strokeplay, he is emerging as one of the world's leading opening batsmen.

Outsiders – but with a growing reputation

The most engaging of all the World Cup teams, Sri Lanka make friends so easily that they could all be employed as ambassadors by the United Nations. Whatever misgivings there may have been about Sri Lanka's elevation to Test status in terms of national strength, their individual reputation as hosts (or as guests, come to that) had been first-class for decades.

They arrived with a growing acclaim as a one-day side, too. In the classic manner of the small army against the large, they had learned quickly to employ their strengths and probe for their opponents' weaknesses; one-day cricket is a form of guerilla warfare, after all.

Core of experience

Although Sri Lanka had played only six Tests on their arrival, their team contained a solid core of first-class experience. Rohan Mendis, the captain, who can bat, bowl and keep wicket, was on his tenth tour in a career that had already taken him to England three times, Pakistan twice, India twice, Zimbabwe, Australia and New Zealand.

Vice-captain Roy Dias boasts a Test batting average of 52 and is a brilliant outfielder, while much English attention focused on Arjuna Ranatunga who, at 19, could emerge as Sri Lanka's first contender for a place in a world XI.

Backbone

Ranjan Madugalle and Sidath Wettimuny have been the backbone of the Sri Lankan batting, the latter scoring 157 against Pakistan in Faisalabad on the recent tour. John Jeyarasingham is only 23 and an all-rounder who can boast five New Zealand wickets for 60, in Wellington. The two reserve batsmen were Athula Samarasekera, 21, who had yet to make an international debut and Susil Fernando who, at 27, gave the side some solidity and experience.

Still at school

Bredon Kuruppu, the reserve wicket-keeper, made his one-day debut against Australia in Colombo, as did the reserve all-rounder, Granville de Silva. Sri Lanka's recognised number one 'keeper is Ronald de Alwis, who has played in two Tests and whose experience is needed to cope with Sri Lanka's versatile and interesting attack.

'Baby' of the party is Rumesh Ratnayake, a fast-medium bowler with three Test caps to his name, yet still at school.

Wins respect

Asantha de Mel arrived with a brisk record as a highly reputable fast-medium bowler (5 for 68 against India in Madras was his best performance) who can move the ball sufficiently to win the respect of the best opposing batsmen. He is no slouch with the bat, averaging 26 in first-class matches.

Until Abdul Qadir appeared in England in 1982, Sri Lanka could claim Somacha de Silva as one of the best exponents of leg-spin and googly bowling. He had the veteran skills of a 38-year-old and some impressive performances ranging from 5 for 59 against Pakistan to 8 for 46 against Oxford University. He could also boast a 97 against Gloucestershire in 1979.

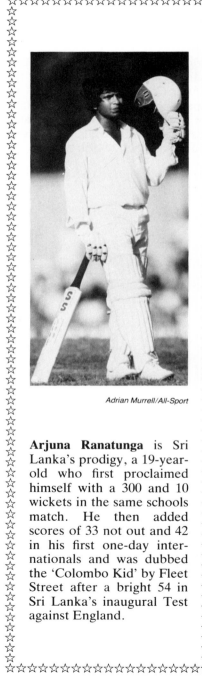

Adrian Murrell/All-Sport

Arjuna Ranatunga is Sri Lanka's prodigy, a 19-year-old who first proclaimed himself with a 300 and 10 wickets in the same schools match. He then added scores of 33 not out and 42 in his first one-day internationals and was dubbed the 'Colombo Kid' by Fleet Street after a bright 54 in Sri Lanka's inaugural Test against England.

More to prove than cricketing ability

Zimbabwe arrived with a political target in mind as much as World Cup glory. Although as Rhodesia, their previous incarnation, they would never have achieved Test status, as the representatives of an internationally recognised and sovereign nation they could make a much more convincing claim.

Behind that claim lay the unspoken thought: would Allan Lamb and Kepler Wessels have had to migrate if they could have won international honours merely by crossing the South African border to play for Zimbabwe? Pie in the sky? Probably. Such a sensible solution would be anathema to the politicians, white or black. Yet it was a hope that stirred Zimbabwe's team into believing that they were in Britain, like the Sri Lankans in 1979, to do more than play cricket.

Not outclassed

Zimbabwe held victories over Young Australia and Sri Lanka. Nor were they outclassed by Young West Indies or by the English county sides in their warm-up games.

The leading fast bowler was Vince Hogg (6 for 26 against Sri Lanka). Duncan Fletcher, their captain, is well known in English cricket. His deputy, John Traicos, is an off-spin bowler of accuracy and stamina and a last-ditch batsman who, while a Rhodesia player, was capped by South Africa against Australia in three Tests in 1970.

Backing Hogg and Fletcher in the seam attack were Peter Rawson and Kevin Curran. The 25-year-old Rawson arrived with first-class credentials, a 63 not out against

Sri Lanka and 13 wickets against Young Australia. Curran, too, was highly regarded as an all-rounder, batting at no. 3 and recording two fine performances against Sri Lanka (96 and 4 for 24).

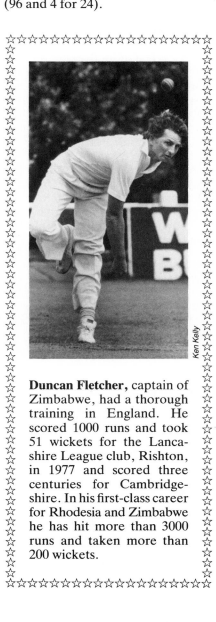

Duncan Fletcher, captain of Zimbabwe, had a thorough training in England. He scored 1000 runs and took 51 wickets for the Lancashire League club, Rishton, in 1977 and scored three centuries for Cambridgeshire. In his first-class career for Rhodesia and Zimbabwe he has hit more than 3000 runs and taken more than 200 wickets.

Ken Kelly

Outstanding batsman

Andy Pycroft, 27, was regarded as the outstanding batsman, developing through South African Universities and Rhodesia. He has hit centuries against Leicestershire and Pakistan International Airlines, was run out for 94 against Young West Indians and then scored 128, 81 and 96 against Sri Lanka.

Jack Heron holds the Currie Cup aggregate record for Rhodesia (747 runs). Ali Shah, the left-handed opener and only non-white player in the team, won his place with scores of 42 and 55 against Young Australia and followed with a century in the second 'Test' against them.

Craig Hodgson, a hard-hitting batsman, was expected to generate some power in the middle order. Grant Paterson batted well against the Young Australians and Ian Butchart's all-round form turned him into a World Cup place candidate on arrival.

Dream player

David Houghton is the one-day captain's dream player, an opening bat who can score quickly and who also keeps wicket to international standards. Strangely, David's deputy, Gerald Peckover, is also a wicketkeeper capable of opening the innings (93 against Eastern Province on debut). There was even a third wicket-keeper in the party, Robin Brown, a sound batsman whose maiden first-class century in the Currie Cup was an undefeated 200.

The batsman in the party bound to attract attention was 17-year-old Graham Hick, Zimbabwe's outstanding schools' player, who arrived in England to make his first-class debut.

Pakistan were the first to appreciate how dangerous Zimbabwe were in limited overs, being beaten by five wickets in a warm-up match at Uxbridge.

Magnificent Lamb gives England impressive start

A pugnacious century from Allan Lamb gave England's campaign a flying launch on election day at the Oval, but brought New Zealand back down to earth with a resounding bump.

Five straight successes over the mother country earlier in the year saw the Kiwis arrive in South London confident that they, not England, would be competing with Pakistan for the two semi-final places open to Group A.

They departed a beaten side in almost every department as England, led by Lamb, slaughtered the New Zealand attack for 322 runs in 60 overs, losing only six wickets in the process. Lamb was the undisputed Man of the Match, with a display of batting that matched his maiden test century scored a year earlier on the same ground against India.

The early-morning pace had been sedate, but after the interval Lamb and Mike Gatting, recalled to England's line-up in place of Derek Randall, led the New Zealand bowlers a merry dance. They added 115 in only 16 overs and inflicted horrendous damage on the morale of New Zealand seamers Martin Snedden and Martin Crowe.

Snedden created a new and inglorious World Cup record by conceding 105 runs in his 12 overs. Crowe was confidently heading for his century but he was pulled out of the firing line after six overs cost 51.

Lamb spiced his 103-delivery century with two sixes, one that took him to 50 and a second, just before a 13-minute break for rain, that hit the pavilion wall only feet from the New Zealand dressing room.

Whirlwind stand

There was more big hitting to come to the delight of the 9,500 crowd as Graham Dilley hit 31 and Mike Gatting 14 in a whirlwind seventh-wicket stand that added 44 in only 3.5 overs before the innings closed.

To score at more than five an over for victory, New Zealand needed runs from their mainline men, but first Edgar fell to a diving catch by wicket-keeper Ian Gould, then Turner was leg-before and Wright miscued a hook into the hands of mid-wicket.

As the middle order folded, the only resistance came from Crowe, a 20-year-old with Bradford League experience, who atoned for his poor bowling with 97 while those around him capitulated.

Graham Dilley is safely home as Warren Lees stretches for a wayward return from the outfield.

Adrian Murrell/All-Sport

Hurried protests

Sadly for the youngster, his innings made as much impact on the highly partisan and excited English crowd as the giant million-pound TV screen specially installed at the Oval for the summer in a Melbourne-style experiment. The modern technology ran into trouble early in the day when, contrary to Test and County Cricket Board instructions it replayed umpire Don Oslear turning down a leg-before appeal against Graeme Fowler.

Hurried protests ensured there were no more repeats of a controversial nature, but the Lancashire left-hander then said the screen had distracted him while the bowling was from the Vauxhall end.

After more consultations it was agreed that the screen be blacked out for left-handers for the rest of the game and so, like New Zealand an expensive experiment also came a cropper.
GO

ENGLAND

G. Fowler, c Coney, b Cairns	
C. J. Tavare, c Edgar, b Chatfield	4
D. I. Gower, c Edgar, b Coney	3
A. J. Lamb, b Snedden	10
M. W. Gatting, b Snedden	4
I. T. Botham, c Lees, b Hadlee	2
†I. J. Gould, not out	1
G. R. Dilley, not out	3
Extras (12 lb, 1 w, 5 nb)	1
60 overs. Total (6 wickets)	322

Did not bat: V. J. Marks, P. J. W. Allott, *R. G. D. Willis.
Fall of wickets: 1-13; 2-79; 3-117; 4-232; 5-271; 6-278.
Bowling: Hadlee 12-4-26-1; Cairns 12-4-57-1; Snedden 12-1-105-2; Chatfield 12-1-45-1; Coney 6-0-20-1; Crowe 6-0-51-0.

NEW ZEALAND

G. M. Turner, lbw, b Willis	1
B. A. Edgar, c Gould, b Willis	
J. G. Wright, c Botham, b Dilley	1
*G. P. Howarth, c Lamb, b Marks	1
J. V. Coney, run out	2
M. D. Crowe, run out	97
†W. K. Lees, b Botham	
R. J. Hadlee, c Lamb, b Marks	
B. L. Cairns, lbw, b Botham	
M. C. Snedden, c Gould, b Gatting	2
E. J. Chatfield, not out	
Extras (2 b, 4 lb, 4 w, 1 nb)	1
59 overs. Total	216

Fall of wickets: 1-3; 2-28; 3-31; 4-62; 5-85; 6-123; 7-136; 8-138; 9-190.
Bowling: Willis 7-2-9-2; Dilley 8-0-33-1; Botham 12-0-42-2; Allott 12-1-47-0; Marks 12-1-39-2; Gatting 8-1-35-1.

Umpires: B. J. Meyer and D. O. Oslear
England won by 106 runs
Man of the match: A. J. LAMB

Historic win for India almost thrown away

India flew in the face of recent form and World Cup history when they beat the holders, West Indies, in their opening match. The shock waves produced by the Indian victory were staggering as West Indies had never before lost a single match in the competition while India had one solitary win hitherto, in 1975, and that against lowly East Africa.

Traditional Old Trafford weather delayed the start beyond lunch, thereby stretching the contest over two days. India's innings was completed on the first and West Indies had received just over a third of their overs, scoring 67 for 2.

West Indies had won the toss and selected to bowl first when a good pitch was at its liveliest and when the light was indifferent. At 76 for 3 in the twenty-second over, the Indian innings wore a forlorn look. With a blend of caution and aggression, Sandeep Patil nursed the innings out of the Intensive Care Unit, if not to blooming health. But Patil first and then the other buccaneer, Kapil Dev, succumbed in thrusting at West Indies' Achilles heel – the fifth bowler. Both got out assaulting Gomes and, at 141 for 5, India were again gasping.

The squat, thickset Yashpal Sharma then stepped into the firing line with crashing off-drives and violent pulls. He stayed until two overs from the innings' statutory end and made 89, with nine fours, having faced 120 balls.

This performance eventually won the Man of the Match award, although not without a challenge from Yashpal's team-mate, Roger Binny, who distinguished himself with both bat and ball. Binny (27)

Bacchus is bowled by Madan Lal and West Indies are in trouble at 96 for 4.

and Madan Lal (21 not out) played no small part in India achieving a total that was defensible.

The match swung West Indies' way as their openers, Greenidge and Haynes put on 49, keeping close enough to the clock in case it rained on the morrow. They scored in quick singles and two's rather than with extravagant shots, and it was not surprising that the stand ended with a run out.

Wide open

At 56, Sandhu got one to nip back at Greenidge and the second day started with the contest wide open. But India soon moved into ascendancy, seizing the wicket of Viv Richards, a potential match-winner. Richards got out to a loose shot at Binny, with the score 76. Bacchus and Dujon betrayed nerves as they

got out to indiscreet blows, reducing West Indies to 107 for 5. Each success lifted the level of India's morale and their outcricket. Even Lloyd could not cut loose.

Desperation led to Gomes being run out and, after a fiercely spinning ball from Shastri accounted for Marshall, Lloyd played a stroke that indicated dejection. A costly fielding lapse gave Holding a second lease and the ninth wicket put on 27. Still, 106 runs remained to be got.

A four and a six by the volatile Garner stampeded Kapil Dev into taking off Shastri, a move which led to India losing control. Kept waiting for so long on the threshold of a momentous win, they came close to panic. With Garner and Roberts playing calmly, even if hitting furiously, the partnership progressed quite effortlessly to 71 before Shastri was recalled to have Garner stumped off his very first ball. **DR**

Dave Cannon/All-Sport

INDIA

S. M. Gavaskar, c Dujon, b Marshall	19
K. Srikkanth, c Dujon, b Holding	14
M. Amarnath, c Dujon, b Garner	21
S. M. Patil, b Gomes	36
Yashpal Sharma, b Holding	89
*Kapil Dev, c Richards, b Gomes	6
R. M. H. Binny, lbw, b Marshall	27
Madan Lal, not out	21
†S. M. H. Kirmani, run out	1
R. J. Shastri, not out	5
Extra (4 b, 10 lb, 1 w, 8 nb)	23

60 overs. Total (8 wickets) 262

Did not bat: B. S. Sandhu.
Fall of wickets: 1-21; 2-46; 3-76; 4-125; 5-141; 6-214; 7-243; 8-246.
Bowling: Holding 12-3-32-2; Roberts 12-1-51-0; Marshall 12-1-48-2; Garner 12-1-49-1; Richards 2-0-13-0; Gomes 10-0-46-2.

WEST INDIES

C. G. Greenidge, b Sandhu	24
D. L. Haynes, run out	24
I. V. A. Richards, c Kirmani, b Binny	17
S. F. A. Bacchus, b Madan Lal	14
*C. H. Lloyd, b Binny	25
†P. J. Dujon, c Sandhu, b Binny	7
H. A. Gomes, run out	8
M. D. Marshall, st Kirmani, b Shastri	2
A. M. E. Roberts, not out	37
M. A. Holding, b Shastri	8
J. Garner, st Kirmani, b Shastri	37
Extras (4 b, 17 lb, 4 w)	25

54.1 overs. Total 228

Fall of wickets: 1-49; 2-56; 3-76; 4-96; 5-107; 6-124; 7-126; 8-130; 9-157.
Bowling: Kapil Dev 10-0-34-0; Sandhu 12-1-36-1; Madan Lal 12-1-34-1; Binny 12-1-48-3; Shastri 5.1-0-26-3; Patil 3-0-25-0.

Umpires: B. Leadbeater and A. G. T. Whitehead
India won by 34 runs
Man of the match: YASHPAL SHARMA

Australia shattered by Fletcher and his men

*P*rivate Eye, Britain's satirical magazine, would have described them as ashen-faced and tight-lipped. Slipping furtively from doorway to doorway, the bookmakers of Britain trembled on the bright morning of June 10: they had accepted odds of 1000-1 against Zimbabwe's winning the World Cup.

The 13-run victory over Australia at Trent Bridge meant that the third Cup tournament began not with a bang but with an explosion. It was a result that excited a public jaded with electioneering and made headline names of players unknown 24 hours earlier.

As the sky darkened after a sunny start, Zimbabwe's openers, sent in by Hughes on a good wicket, found it difficult to do much more than survive. Ali Shah was dropped when 11 by Wessels off Hogg and, although the rate quickened when Lillee ap-

peared, it was the veteran who struck, removing both openers with successive deliveries at 55, after 18 overs.

The unrated Yallop then sent back Heron and Houghton with successive balls while Pycroft fell immediately before lunch when 94 for 5, off 33 overs, had to be read as impending defeat.

Enter Duncan Fletcher. The Zimbabwe captain first added 70 in 15 overs with Curran, then another 75 in 12 overs with Butchart. The famous Australian pace attack suddenly looked blunted and middle-aged although, with five catches going down, they had good reason to be disappointed.

Solid start

Wood and Wessels gave Australia a solid start of 61, Zimbabwe proving they had done their homework.

They pinned down Wessels on hi leg stump instead of feeding his off side shots, as England did so often ir Australia.

Enter Fletcher again. Wood wa caught behind, Hughes added to hi long list of English failures, Hooke: was beautifully taken at cover Yallop fell to an acrobatic boundary catch and the first shiver wen through a continent when Wessels the rock, was shattered by Heron' fast and accurate throw that ran him out.

With wickets falling and time run ning out Australia had no alternative but death or glory; even Marsh, the battle-scarred rearguard commander accepted with 53 needed and only 3(balls to be bowled that there wasn' enough ammunition left.

Fletcher finished with 69 not ou and 4 for 42 in his 11 overs, truly the Man of the Match. There must have been many of his old friends up ir the Lancashire League cheerin; their heads off.   **DI**

Steve Powell/All-Sport

Rod Marsh watches anxiously as Man of the Match Duncan Fletcher hits out.

ZIMBABWE

A. H. Shah, c Marsh, b Lillee	1
G. A. Paterson, c Hookes, b Lillee	2
J. G. Heron, c Marsh, b Yallop	1
A. J. Pycroft, b Border	2
†D. L. Houghton, c Marsh, b Yallop	
*D. A. G. Fletcher, not out	6
K. M. Curran, c Hookes, b Hogg	3
I. Butchart, not out	3
Extras (18 lb, 7 w, 6 nb)	3

60 overs. Total (6 wickets) 23

Did not bat: P. W. E. Rawson, A. J. Traicos, V. R Hogg.
Fall of wickets: 1-55; 2-55; 3-86; 4-86; 5-9 6-164.
Bowling: Lawson 11-2-33-0; Hogg 12-3-43- Lillee 12-1-47-2; Thomson 11-1-46-0; Yallo 9-0-28-2; Border 5-0-11-1.

AUSTRALIA

G. M. Wood, c Houghton, b Fletcher	3
K. C. Wessels, run out	7
*K. J. Hughes, c Shah, b Fletcher	
D. W. Hookes, c Traicos, b Fletcher	2
G. N. Yallop, c Pycroft, b Fletcher	
A. R. Border, c Pycroft, b Curran	1
†R. W. Marsh, not out	5
G. F. Lawson, b Butchart	
R. M. Hogg, not out	1
Extras (2 b, 7 lb, 2 w)	1

60 overs. Total (7 wickets) 22

Did not bat: D. K. Lillee, J. R. Thomson.
Fall of wickets: 1-61; 2-63; 3-114; 4-133; 5-13 6-168; 7-176.
Bowling: Hogg 6-2-15-0; Rawson 12-1-54- Butchart 10-0-39-1; Fletcher 11-1-42-4; Traicc 12-2-27-0; Curran 9-0-38-1.

Umpires: D. J. Constant and M. J. Kitchen
Zimbabwe won by 13 runs
Man of the match: D. A. G. FLETCHER

Records tumble as Sri Lankan bowlers suffer

Pakistan, with pre-competition worries over the loss of the bowling skills of their captain Imran Khan, could hardly have made a more impressive start, setting a new Prudential World Cup record with their total of 338 for 5. Sri Lanka certainly played their full part, for their reply of 288 for 9 was also a record for a side batting second, and the match aggregate of 626 runs improved by 22 the previous highest, scored in a 1975 match in which Sri Lanka lost to the Australians.

Although Sri Lanka were able to bat in warm sunshine under cloudless blue skies and on a slow wicket that gave the bowlers no help, they were never in with a serious chance of overhauling the massive target.

Pakistan, sent in by Duleep Mendis on a damp, slow pitch, took some time to acclimatise, but once Mudassar and Mohsin – later named Man of the Match – had established a platform with an opening stand of 88 in 26 overs, it was a story of steady acceleration and a dynamic finish, with 108 runs coming from the final ten overs and 72 from the last five.

It was, appropriately, Imran who led the final surge with a dazzling 56 not out, made off just 33 balls. One of the two sixes he hit off the unfortunate John enabled Pakistan to reach the new record. Two overs earlier he had blasted John for 22 runs – four fours and a six from consecutive balls – and the medium-pacer, who conceded only 16 runs from his first nine overs, was put to the sword with 42 coming off him in his last three.

Javed Miandad, delighting his Glamorgan followers, shared in the late slaughter, making 72 from 54 balls, with three huge sixes off Asantha de Mel. His partnership with Imran raised 96 in nine overs.

Benign conditions

Pakistan's attack in the absence of Imran, under doctor's orders not to bowl on his injured right shin, looked moderate in the benign batting conditions and 21-year-old opener Brendon Kuruppu took advantage to hit an attractive 72 in 33 overs with two sixes and seven fours before he was fourth out at 142, run out by a throw from Zaheer at mid wicket.

Sri Lanka did well to keep pace with the Pakistan scoring rate, with Somachandra de Silva and Guy de Alwis sharing a useful eighth-wicket stand of 54 in 11 overs following a middle-order slump. De Alwis was still there at the end with an unbeaten 59.   **RD**

PAKISTAN

Mudassar Nazar, c D. S. de Silva, b Ratnayake...	36
Mohsin Khan, b John	82
Zaheer Abbas, c Kuruppu, b de Mel	82
Javed Miandad, lbw, b de Mel	72
*Imran Khan not out	56
Ijaz Fakih, run out	2
Tahir Naqqash, not out	0
Extras (4 b, 4 lb)	8
60 overs. Total (5 wickets)	338

Did not bat: †Wasim Bari, Rashid Khan, Shahid Mahboob, Sarfraz Nawaz.
Fall of wickets: 1-88; 2-156; 3-229; 4-325; 5-332.
Bowling: de Mel 12-2-69-2; John 12-2-58-1; Ratnayake 12-0-65-1; Ranatunga 9-0-53-0; D. S. de Silva 10-0-52-0; Samarasekera 5-0-33-0.

SRI LANKA

S. Wettimuny, c Rashid, b Sarfraz	12
B. Kuruppu, run out	72
R. L. Dias, b Rashid	5
*R. L. D. Mendis, b Tahir	16
A. Ranatunga, c and b Mudassar	31
M. A. R. Samarasekera, run out	0
D. S. de Silva, c Wasim Bari, b Sarfraz	35
A. L. F. de Mel, c Tahir, b Shahid	11
†R. G. de Alwis, not out	59
R. J. Ratnayake, c Mudassar, b Sarfraz	13
V. B. John, not out	12
Extras (8 lb, 10 w, 4 nb)	22
60 overs. Total (9 wickets)	288

Fall of wickets: 1-34; 2-58; 3-85; 4-142; 5-143; 6-157; 7-180; 8-234; 9-262.
Bowling: Sarfraz 12-1-40-3; Shahid 11-0-48-1; Tahir 8-0-49-1; Rashid 12-1-55-1; Ijaz 12-1-52-0; Mudassar 4-0-18-1; Zaheer 1-0-4-0.

Umpires: K. E. Palmer and D. R. Shepherd.

Pakistan won by 50 runs
Man of the match: MOHSIN KHAN

Mohsin Khan paddles one round the corner during his innings of 82. De Alwis is the wicket-keeper.

Magnificent Gower leads England run-feast

Wettimuny looks anxiously towards the slips after playing a rising ball from Dilley.

England emerged as World Cup favourites with a second successive group victory. David Gower, who earned the Man of the Match award for a superb century, Vic Marks, with a five-wickets performance, and Graham Dilley, with an effective all-round showing, were the men who spearheaded the success by 47 runs over the fighting Sri Lankans, with valuable contributions from Allan Lamb and Ian Gould.

The elegant Leicestershire left-hander showed an aggressive determination as he hit 130 from only 120 balls, with five sixes and 12 fours. Three of the sixes were beautifully struck hits over long-on to the sumptuous new Taunton pavilion area, two of them coming from successive deliveries from Ratnayake.

Faltered

The innings faltered with two run-outs in the space of four balls in the forty-third and forty-fourth overs, with Gatting and Somerset's own favourite son, Ian Botham, the victims of Gower's somewhat ill-judged calling for second runs. For Botham, out for a duck after receiving just one delivery, it was a particularly bitter pill to swallow in front of his own crowd.

Gower was bowled swinging out at de Mel at 292, but England's late order continued to keep the runs flowing, mainly through Dilley, who smote the ball beefily for a 29 that included five fours and was made off just 17 deliveries. The last ten overs raised 105 runs, with 55 from the final five.

The Sri Lankans hardly looked ready to justify Sir Gary Sobers' confident assertion that 'they will chase any target' when their first two wickets fell for 17 by the sixth over, with a rampant Dilley claiming both. He sent back a nervous Brendon Kuruppu in his opening over and then dismissed Roy Dias thanks to a spectacular flying catch at second slip by Botham, gaining consolation for his other disappointments of the day.

But the Sri Lankan captain, Duleep Mendis, aided by an unruffled Sidath Wettimuny, set about restoring the damage and in fact ensured that their side's rate stayed ahead of England's at that stage. Mendis hooked Willis for a six to the new pavilion and Wettimuny repeated the shot off Botham, who was to have an unhappy time with the ball as well, returning 0 for 60.

Marks, bowling well to his field, captured both their wickets and completed his 12-overs spell with an impressive 5 for 39 return.

There was still defiance to come from Sri Lanka, however, with de Mel joining Guy de Alwis in a half-century stand in only seven overs. England's attack was showing signs of wear, with Paul Allott especially unimpressive (he conceded 82 runs for de Mel's wicket in his 12 overs), but Dilley came back to dismiss Ratnayake and John in the fifty-eighth over and end the Sri Lanka innings at 286, two short of their record score against Pakistan. **RD**

ENGLAND	
G. Fowler, b John	22
C. J. Tavare, c de Alwis, b Ranatunga	32
D. I. Gower, b de Mel	130
A. J. Lamb, b Ratnayake	53
M. W. Gatting, run out	7
I. T. Botham, run out	0
†I. J. Gould, c Ranatunga, b Ratnayake	35
G. R. Dilley, b de Mel	29
V. J. Marks, run out	5
P. J. W. Allott, not out	0
Extras (11 lb, 8 w, 1 nb)	20
60 overs. Total (9 wickets)	333

Did not bat: *R. G. D. Willis.
Fall of wickets: 1-49; 2-78; 3-174; 4-193; 5-194; 6-292; 7-298; 8-333; 9-333.
Bowling: de Mel 12-3-62-2; John 12-0-55-1; Ratnayake 12-0-66-2; Ranatunga 12-0-65-1; de Silva 12-0-65-0.

SRI LANKA	
S. Wettimuny, lbw, b Marks	33
B. Kuruppu, c Gatting, b Dilley	4
R. L. Dias, c Botham, b Dilley	2
*R. L. D. Mendis, c Willis, b Marks	56
R. S. Madugalle, c Tavare, b Marks	12
A. Ranatunga, c Lamb, b Marks	34
D. S. de Silva, st Gould, b Marks	28
†R. G. de Alwis, not out	58
A. L. F. de Mel, c Dilley, b Allott	27
R. J. Ratnayake, c Lamb, b Dilley	15
V. B. John, b Dilley	0
Extras (12 lb, 2 w, 3 nb)	17
58 overs. Total	286

Fall of wickets: 1-11; 2-17; 3-92; 4-108; 5-117 6-168; 7-192; 8-246; 9-281.
Bowling: Willis 11-3-43-0; Dilley 11-0-45-4; Allott 12-1-82-1; Botham 12-0-60-0; Marks 12-3-39-5.

Umpires: M. J. Kitchen and K. E. Palmer
England won by 47 runs   **Man of the match: D. I. GOWER**

Poor batting helps Hadlee tear Pakistan apart

Few score-flashes in the Prudential Cup series were as unexpected as the agency message from Edgbaston: Pakistan 0 for 3 after 1.2 overs. In the space of eight deliveries, Richard Hadlee and Lance Cairns had re-shaped a match which was largely in Pakistan's control until they lapsed into an abject reply to New Zealand's 238 for 9.

Recriminations were immediate after Pakistan had been bowled out for 186 on a completely blameless pitch. Imran Khan, their captain, criticised his batsmen – presumably including himself for a reckless shot which gave Hadlee his third wicket – and said later: 'When the sun came out, there was no way we should have lost. All we wanted was a start.'

Unfortunately, Imran allowed his displeasure to fan the flames of controversy by rebuking umpire Barrie Leadbeater for upholding an lbw appeal when Hadlee rapped Mohsin Khan at knee height on the front pad. 'It was a terrible decision and I am not embarrassed to say so,' commented Imran. The issue should have been confined to private debate. The scale of the Pakistan collapse was not influenced by outside factors, other than that Hadlee bowled superbly and that New Zealand's supporting seamers, notably Jeremy Coney's gentle outswingers, held the original bridgehead.

Mysterious Qadir

The only consolation for Pakistan came when their last four batsmen added 97 in an entertaining phase which clinched Abdul Qadir's nomination as Man of the Match by M. J. K. Smith. In his first appearance in the Prudential Cup, he took 4 for 21 in 12 marvellous overs in which every batsman appeared to be transfixed by a never-ending variety of leg-breaks, top-spinners and googlies.

Geoff Howarth, the New Zealand captain, probably captured the general reaction perfectly when he was asked to comment from the batsmen's point of view. He replied in one word: 'Mysterious'.

New Zealand may have underestimated Qadir, and certainly they were hasty in promoting Cairns, who might have been better employed later against a modest medium-paced attack.

Impressive prospect

In the event, New Zealand lost half their side for 120 in the rain-interrupted Saturday, and got that far only because Bruce Edgar registered the top score in the match, 44, after giving three chances in his vulnerable area around the off stump. Coney and the impressive 20-year-old prospect, Martin Crowe, managed to retrieve the situation on Saturday evening, and Warren Lees made the most of four overs spilling into a second day on Sunday.

Pakistan were still unconcerned at that stage on a ground where the side batting second is favoured to reach a total of anything up to 300 in 60 overs. But this was to be an exception to the general rule at Edgbaston. **MB**

NEW ZEALAND

G. M. Turner, c Wasim Bari, b Rashid	27
B. A. Edgar, c Imran, b Qadir	44
J. G. Wright, c Wasim Bari, b Qadir	9
D. L. Cairns, b Qadir	4
*G. P. Howarth, st Wasim Bari, b Qadir	16
J. V. Coney, c Ijaz, b Shahid	33
M. D. Crowe, c Mohsin, b Rashid	34
R. J. Hadlee, c Wasim Bari, b Sarfraz	13
J. G. Bracewell, lbw, b Rashid	3
†W. K. Lees, not out	24
E. J. Chatfield, not out	6
Extras (20 lb, 4 w, 1 nb)	25
60 overs. Total (9 wickets)	238

Fall of wickets: 1-57; 2-68; 3-80; 4-109; 5-120; 6-166; 7-197; 8-202; 9-223.
Bowling: Sarfraz 11-1-49-1; Shahid 10-2-38-1; Rashid 11-0-47-3; Mudassar 12-1-40-0; Qadir 12-4-21-4; Ijaz 1-0-6-0; Zaheer 3-0-12-0.

PAKISTAN

Mohsin Khan, lbw, b Hadlee	0
Mudassar Nazar, c Lees, b Cairns	0
Zaheer Abbas, b Hadlee	0
Javed Miandad, lbw, b Chatfield	35
*Imran Khan, c Chatfield, b Hadlee	9
Ijaz Fakih, c Edgar, b Coney	12
Shahid Mahboob, c Wright, b Coney	17
†Wasim Bari, c Edgar, b Coney	34
Abdul Qadir, not out	41
Sarfraz Nawaz, c Crowe, b Chatfield	13
Rashid Khan, c and b Cairns	9
Extras (5 b, 6 lb, 3 w, 2 nb)	16
55.2 overs. Total	186

Fall of wickets: 1-0; 2-0; 3-0; 4-22; 5-54; 6-60; 7-102; 8-135; 9-158.
Bowling: Hadlee 9-2-20-3; Cairns 9.2-3-21-2; Chatfield 12-0-50-2; Crowe 2-0-12-0; Coney 12-3-28-3; Bracewell 11-2-39-0.

Umpires: H. D. Bird and B. Leadbeater

New Zealand won by 52 runs
Man of the match: ABDUL QADIR

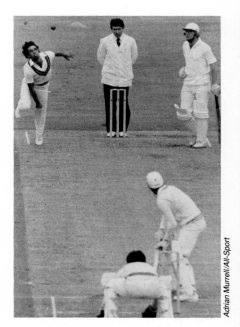

Man of the Match Abdul Qadir weaves his magic.

Adrian Murrell/All-Sport

19

Australians blame wicket as Davis sets new record

He may have been Winston Who? at 10.45 on a sunny Sunday morning at Leeds, but 24 hours later the *Daily Express* was proclaiming 'The Davis Cup'. The 6' 6" tall, 24-year-old St Vincent and Glamorgan fast bowler, a former worker in a flour mill, gave the world a delightfully innocent grin when Brian Close rightfully proclaimed him Man of the Match.

This was an always tense and dramatic contest, won in the end by West Indies by the large margin of 101. Both teams had been beaten in their opening matches, nor could

they get to grips until 3.30 on the Saturday afternoon as a belt of black cloud and intermittent rain crossed Leeds.

Hughes decided eventually that West Indies should bat; the ball seamed awkwardly and bounced variably and a few of the eminent professors on view showed their disgust all too plainly. Lawson bowled superbly for Australia, his best support coming mainly from the newcomer MacLeay, whose medium-fast attack looked well suited to English conditions.

Too many extras

Application and graft were needed by the batsmen and Gomes, who did spend three years with Middlesex, showed those qualities in an innings that was eventually to spread over 47 overs for 78 runs that may not have contained too many brilliant strokes but, in their way, were as valuable as Davis's contribution.

The Australians, for the second time, conceded 31 extras in a match, the equivalent in wides and no-balls of a gift of 3½ overs to the opposition. By Sunday morning the West Indies' tail was swinging merrily and a target of 253 was thought to be perhaps 30 runs too many for Australia.

Even 150 began to look like a mountain when, in Holding's second over, Wood ducked to a short ball that did not rise as he expected. He

took a blow on the right side of the face, was knocked unconscious for seconds and eventually spent a night in hospital suffering from concussion.

Bitter comments

Australia made some bitter comments about the wicket afterwards but the fact remains that their batsmen panicked. Hughes, hooking the first two balls from Daniel for six, Hookes and Yallop all played some superb shots and 88 runs came in 10

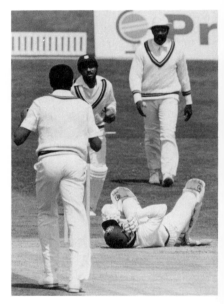

Contrasting fortunes. *Above:* Graeme Wood goes down, severely concussed by a ball from Holding. *Below:* His team-mates share seven-wicket Winston Davis's obvious delight as Border is dismissed.

WEST INDIES

C. G. Greenidge, c Wood, b Hogg	4
D. L. Haynes, c Marsh, b Lawson	13
I. V. A. Richards, b Lawson	7
H. A. Gomes, c Marsh, b Lillee	78
*C. H. Lloyd, lbw, b MacLeay	19
S. F. A. Bacchus, c Wessels, b Yallop	47
†P. J. Dujon, lbw, b Lawson	12
A. M. E. Roberts, c Marsh, b Lillee	5
M. A. Holding, run out	20
W. W. Daniels, not out	16
Extras (1 b, 9 lb, 10 w, 11 nb)	31
60 overs. Total (9 wickets)	252

Did not bat: W. W. Davis.
Fall of wickets: 1-7; 2-25; 3-32; 4-78; 5-156; 6-192; 7-208; 8-211; 9-252.
Bowling: Lawson 12-3-29-3; Hogg 12-1-49-1; MacLeay 12-1-31-1; Lillee 12-0-55-2; Yallop 5-0-26-1; Border 7-0-31-0.

AUSTRALIA

G. M. Wood, retired hurt	2
K. C. Wessels, b Roberts	11
*K. J. Hughes, c Lloyd, b Davis	18
D. W. Hookes, c Dujon, b Davis	45
G. N. Yallop, c Holding, b Davis	29
A. R. Border, c Lloyd, b Davis	17
K. H. MacLeay, c Haynes, b Davis	1
*R. W. Marsh, c Haynes, b Holding	8
G. F. Lawson, c Dujon, b Davis	2
R. M. Hogg, not out	0
D. K. Lillee, b Davis	0
Extras (1 b, 4 lb, 5 w, 8 nb)	18
30.3 overs. Total	151

Fall of wickets: 1-18; 2-55; 3-114; 4-116; 5-126; 6-137; 7-141; 8-150; 9-151.
Bowling: Roberts 7-0-14-1; Holding 8-2-23-1; Davis 10.3-0-51-7; Daniel 3-0-35-0; Gomes 2-0-10-0.

Umpires: D. J. Constant and D. G. L. Evans.
West Indies won by 101 runs
Man of the match: W. W. DAVIS

One-sided disappointment

Geoff Lawson's joy is understandable as he knocks back the off stump of the great Viv Richards.

overs after lunch, but it was a brittle glory.

Lloyd, reluctant to bring back Holding or Roberts too soon, without the injured Garner and Marshall, and having seen Daniel hit for 35 in three overs, kept Davis on at the fast bowler's end, from Kirkstall Lane.

His first five overs had cost 37 runs for Hughes's wicket. His next 33 deliveries produced six wickets for 14 runs: he ran in well, he bowled quick and straight, and the wicket, with Australian desperation, did the rest.

Once again Leeds was a disaster for Australia. 'I've played here five times and have yet to play on a good wicket' was Hughes's comment.

Davis's 7 for 51 became the new best analysis in the World Cup, overtaking Gary Gilmour's 6 for 14 for Australia against England in 1975. That happened, of course, at Headingley. **DH**

The battle of the giant-killers, at Grace Road, proved a damp squib, Zimbabwe falling below the expectations they had raised by beating Australia in the previous round of matches. The contest was so one-sided that the issue was settled in a day in spite of rain having delayed the start until 1.25 pm.

The impressive margin of the Indians' victory masked the fact that they themselves did not perform with the resolution and discipline in the field that enabled them to bring down the mighty West Indies on the previous day. Their fielding was redeemed only by Kirmani, who established a new wicket-keeping record for the competition by taking five catches.

There were only two partnerships of any substance during the Zimbabwe innings. The first was for the second wicket between Grant Paterson and Jack Heron, who put on 42, and then a fifth-wicket stand between David Houghton and

Jack Heron looks apprehensive but survived this lbw appeal.

the skipper, left-handed Duncan Fletcher, raised 35.

The Zimbabwean attack was depleted by injuries to two front-line bowlers. Vince Hogg, prominent for his economy in the match against Australia, was a non-starter because of a back injury. Peter Rawson, who took on the mantle of spearhead, was similarly afflicted just after he had disposed of both Indian openers and was leading a spirited Zimbabwe recovery.

Patil and Amarnath staged the match-winning partnership of 69 in 16 overs. It was surprising that India did not endeavour to raise their scoring rate by Kapil Dev promoting himself in the batting order. **DR**

ZIMBABWE

A. H. Shah, c Kirmani, b Sandhu	8
G. A. Paterson, lbw, b Madan Lal	22
J. G. Heron, c Kirmani, b Madan Lal	18
A. J. Pycroft, c Shastri, b Binny	14
D. L. Houghton, c Kirmani, b Madan Lal	21
*D. A. G. Fletcher, b Kapil Dev	13
K. M. Curran, run out	8
I. Butchart, not out	22
†R. D. Brown, c Kirmani, b Shastri	6
P. W. E. Rawson, c Kirmani, b Binny	3
A. J. Traicos, run out	2
Extras (9 lb, 9 w)	18

51.4 overs. Total 155

Fall of wickets: 1-13; 2-55; 3-56; 4-71; 5-106; 6-114; 7-115; 8-139; 9-148.
Bowling: Kapil Dev 9-3-18-1; Sandhu 9-1-29-1; Madan Lal 10.4-0-27-3; Binny 11-2-25-2; Shastri 12-1-38-1.

INDIA

S. Srikkanth, c Butchart, b Rawson	20
S. M. Gavaskar, c Heron, b Rawson	4
M. Amarnath, c sub, b Traicos	44
S. M. Patil, b Fletcher	50
R. J. Shastri, c Brown, b Shah	17
Yashpal Sharma, not out	18
*Kapil Dev, not out	2
Extras (2 w)	2

37.3 overs. Total (5 wickets) 157

Did not bat: Madan Lal, †S. M. H. Kirmani, B. S. Sandhu, R. M. Binny.
Fall of wickets: 1-13; 2-32; 3-101; 4-128; 5-148.
Bowling: Rawson 5.1-1-11-2; Curran 6.5-1-33-0; Butchart 5-1-21-0; Traicos 11-1-41-1; Fletcher 6-1-32-1; Shah 3.3-0-17-1.

Umpires: J. Birkenshaw and R. Palmer
India won by 5 wickets
Man of the match: MADAN LAL

Pakistan no match for England's efficiency

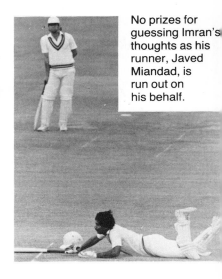

No prizes for guessing Imran's thoughts as his runner, Javed Miandad, is run out on his behalf.

Pakistan arrived at Lord's backed by vociferous supporters in the capacity 25,000 crowd and an awesome batting reputation that had seen them set a new World Cup record of 338 only four days earlier. They departed eight hours later soundly beaten and desperately lacking the penetrative bowling of their injured captain, Imran Khan.

For the first time in the competition Bob Willis lost the toss, but he was not to regret it as Pakistan took the perilous course of batting first on a lively, bouncy wicket.

Mohsin Khan and Mudassar Nazar nervously negotiated the opening ten overs against a determined Willis and speedy Graham Dilley. Had they survived the blast, the result might have been different after the mediocre bowling performances of England's Paul Allott and Ian Botham against New Zealand and Sri Lanka.

Graceful Zaheer

Willis, however, gave himself an extended spell of 12 overs and mercilessly dispatched Mohsin and Mansoor Akhtar back to the pavilion with only 33 runs on the board. Botham found his long-lost line and length to see off Javed Miandad and Wasim Raja, while Allott had the stubborn Mudassar Nazar caught at the wicket after struggling for 31 overs over 26.

Only Zaheer Abbas, graceful in defence and powerful in attack, prevented Pakistan from a score of disaster proportions. He earned the Man of the Match award for his 83 not out that took his side to 193 for 8 when their overs ran out. The award was adjudicated by former England wicket-keeper, John Murray.

Facing a target of just above three runs an over, England set about their task with a cool determination that may not have excited the huge crowd but clearly demonstrated a renewed professional attitude.

There was a hiccup when Chris Tavare fell leg-before to Rashid Khan in the ninth over with only 15 runs in the bank, but Graeme Fowler, after two earlier failures in the competition, took advantage of the leisurely pace required to repro-duce the early-season form he had displayed with Lancashire.

Confident Gower

For a time it looked quite on the cards that David Gower, fresh from his 130 at Taunton at the weekend, would win the match single-handed. Confidence oozed from his bat as he raced to 48 before he was second to go at 93, brilliantly caught by Sarfraz Nawaz diving to his right at mid-wicket off the bowling of Mansoor.

With Abdul Qadir attempting to bamboozle the English batsmen with his crafty mixture of leg-breaks and googlies, there was still a chance that Pakistan might stem the tide. Allan Lamb twice failed to read Qadir's 'wrong 'un' soon after arriving at the crease, but there was no bowling support on hand.

Fowler switched into top gear and, despite his known distaste for the one-day games, played himself into form with 78 not out.

Lamb simply decided to belt his way out of trouble and finished the match for England with 56 balls to spare with a straight six off Qadir that took his own total to 48 not out for a tournament aggregate of 203 from three visits to the crease (once not out). **GO**

PAKISTAN

Mohsin Khan, c Tavare, b Willis	3
Mudassar Nazar, c Gould, b Allott	26
Mansoor Akhtar, c Gould, b Willis	3
Javed Miandad, c Gould, b Botham	14
Zaheer Abbas, not out	83
*Imran Khan, run out	7
Wasim Raja, c Botham, b Marks	9
Abdul Qadir, run out	0
Sarfraz Nawaz, c and b Botham	11
†Wasim Bari, not out	18
Extras (5 b, 8 lb, 3 w, 3 nb)	19
60 overs. Total (8 wickets)	193

Did not bat: Rashid Khan.
Fall of wickets: 1-29; 2-33; 3-49; 4-67; 5-96; 6-112; 7-118; 8-154.
Bowling: Willis 12-4-24-2; Dilley 12-1-33-0; Allott 12-2-48-1; Botham 12-3-36-2; Marks 12-1-33-1.

ENGLAND

G. Fowler, not out	78
C. J. Tavare, lbw, b Rashid	8
D. I. Gower, c Sarfraz, b Mansoor	48
A. J. Lamb, not out	48
Extras (1 b, 12 lb, 2 w, 2 nb)	17
50.4 overs. Total (2 wickets)	199

Did not bat: M. W. Gatting, I. T. Botham, †I. J. Gould, V. J. Marks, G. R. Dilley, P. J. W. Allott, *R. G. D. Willis.
Fall of wickets: 1-15; 2-93.
Bowling: Rashid 7-2-19-1; Sarfraz 11-5-22-0; Wasim Raja 3-0-14-0; Mudassar 8-0-30-0; Qadir 9.4-0-53-0; Mansoor 12-2-44-1.
Umpires: B. J. Meyer and A. G. T. Whitehead
England won by 8 wickets
Man of the match: ZAHEER ABBAS

Zimbabwe outgunned but earn West Indies' respect

Perhaps the highest compliment that can be paid to Zimbabwe – and one which their players will certainly treasure – is that they earned the total respect of the world champions in a fascinating and at times exciting match at Worcester.

Gordon Greenidge has not often completed a 50 with only one boundary and probably he can't recall too many occasions when he has scored an unbeaten 105 with only five fours and a six. 'They made us fight for every run,' acknowledged Greenidge after he had pipped Zimbabwe's captain, Duncan Fletcher, for the Man of the Match award.

Fletcher is a stylish left-hander with a temperament suited to leading his side out of awkward situations. As he had done against Australia at Trent Bridge, he transformed the game by making an undefeated 71 after Zimbabwe had used up half their overs in reaching 65 for 4.

Achilles heel

The growth of the innings had been stunted, as one might have

Duncan Fletcher: all concentration and determination.

Dave Cannon/All-Sport

expected, by West Indies' formidable pace quartet. The unfortunate Jack Heron took 41 minutes to get off the mark and scored only 12 off 73 balls, creating pressure which led to Andrew Pycroft being run out by a brilliant piece of fielding by Viv Richards.

But Fletcher and the purposeful David Houghton took advantage of West Indies' Achilles heel – 12 overs of spin from Gomes and Richards. Those overs provided 55 of the 92 runs added for the fifth wicket, and with two batsmen fully adjusted to the pace of the pitch, the quick bowlers did not have their earlier impact. Although Houghton fell to an away-swinger from Andy Roberts for 54, Fletcher stayed to the end, nursing Zimbabwe to an acceptable total of 217 for 7.

West Indies were immediately disrupted by two stoppages for bad light, and there was just a suggestion that their composure was ruffled in an aggressive opening spell by the fast-medium Peter Rawson. He had happy memories of taking five wickets against Worcestershire at New Road in 1982; now, a big outswinger accounted for Haynes and one going the other way pinned Richards on the back foot.

Magnificent fielding

West Indies were then 23 for 2 and finding it difficult to shake themselves loose from Zimbabwe's magnificent standard of ground fielding. But the minnows' dream of capturing another world-class scalp slowly subsided as Greenidge drew on his vast experience of one-day cricket in England with Hampshire.

Zimbabwe's ability to cut off the boundaries was countered by Greenidge and Gomes running their singles with outstanding judgment. Nothing is more irritating for the fielding side and, once the third-wicket pair had stabilised the innings, the tide became a flood.

Gomes improved steadily after an insecure start, when he was swishing recklessly outside his off stump, while Greenidge imposed his high quality in a costly period of spin bowling by John Traicos and Ali Shah. They remained unbeaten and their partnership of 195 was a record for any wicket in the Prudential Cup. **MB**

ZIMBABWE	
A. H. Shah, b Roberts	2
G. A. Paterson, c Dujon, b Holding	4
J. G. Heron, st Dujon, b Gomes	12
A. J. Pycroft, run out	13
†D. L. Houghton, c Dujon, b Roberts	54
*D. A. G. Fletcher, not out	71
K. M. Curran, b Roberts	7
I. Butchart, lbw, b Holding	0
G. E. Peckover, not out	16
Extras (1 b, 23 lb, 7 w, 7 nb)	38
60 overs. Total (7 wickets)	217

Did not bat: P. W. E. Rawson, A. J. Traicos.
Fall of wickets: 1-7; 2-7; 3-35; 4-65; 5-157; 6-181; 7-183.
Bowling: Roberts 12-4-36-3; Holding 12-2-33-2; Daniel 12-4-21-0; Davis 12-2-34-0; Gomes 8-0-42-1; Richards 4-1-13-0.

WEST INDIES	
C. G. Greenidge, not out	105
D. L. Haynes, c Houghton, b Rawson	2
I. V. A. Richards, lbw, b Rawson	16
H. A. Gomes, not out	75
Extras (1 b, 8 lb, 9 w, 2 nb)	20
48.3 overs. Total (2 wickets)	218

Did not bat: S. F. A. Bacchus, *C. H. Lloyd, †P. J. Dujon, W. W. Daniel, A. M. E. Roberts, M. A. Holding, W. W. Davis.
Fall of wickets: 1-3; 2-23.
Bowling: Rawson 12-1-39-2; Curran 10.3-1-37-0; Butchart 9-1-40-0; Fletcher 4-0-22-0; Traicos 9-0-37-0; Shah 4-0-23-0.
Umpires: D. G. L. Evans and J. Birkenshaw

West Indies won by 8 wickets
Man of the match: C. G. GREENIDGE

No places for Lillee or Gavaskar in one-sided game

From the fourth over of the match, when Trevor Chappell and Kim Hughes came together for a second-wicket partnership of 144, Australia's fortunes were always rising. The one-sided nature of the match and the margin of 162 runs belied the earlier record in the competition of the rivals – India, two wins from two matches; Australia, two losses in two matches.

There was no room in the Australian side for an off-form Dennis Lillee, who was replaced by the quickish left-arm spinner, Tom Hogan. The Indians ignored Sunil Gavaskar's reputation and glorious past in view of his poor current form and his lack of mobility in the field.

The day was bright and clear to start with, damp and murky afterwards. The Australian innings occupied the summery part of it. The Indian bowling, apart from Kapil Dev and the loyal Madan Lal, was not good enough to contain Australian ebullience in such lovely batting conditions.

The supporting bowlers were so inadequate that, for the first time, Kapil Dev had to turn to a seventh bowler. The Indians, moreover, did not help themselves by dropping chances. Chappell, who otherwise played quite brilliantly and was voted Man of the Match, should have been caught at 27 and 71. Border also had two escapes.

In hitting 13 fours, Chappell's most telling strokes were square cuts, drives through extra cover and crisp, typically Australian flicks off the legs. Hughes participated very actively in his stand with Chappell by placing the ball neatly into gaps and running superbly between the wickets. When Madan Lal deceived Hookes with a slower ball, the Indians were spared an onslaught from the brilliant left-hander, but by then Yallop had them by the scruff.

Srikkanth, with his dazzling unorthodox strokeplay, hit five fours in the first six overs of India's innings, which produced 38 runs. But from that point the Indians went into a nose-dive. MacLeay, who took six wickets for 39, struck three times in his first four overs, each wicket costing only one run.

India were 66 for 6 in the twenty-second over before they recovered even somewhat, with Kapil Dev and Madan Lal striking out to add 58 in nine overs. But by then, the fate of the match had long been sealed. **DR**

Runs for Srikkanth, consternation for Marsh, during the Indian opener's 39.

AUSTRALIA

K. C. Wessels, b Kapil Dev	5
T. M. Chappell, c Srikkanth, b Amarnath	110
*K. J. Hughes, b Madan Lal	52
D. W. Hookes, c Kapil Dev, b Madan Lal	1
G. N. Yallop, not out	66
A. R. Border, c Yashpal Sharma, b Binny	26
†R. W. Marsh, c Sandhu, b Kapil Dev	12
K. H. MacLeay, c and b Kapil Dev	4
T. G. Hogan, b Kapil Dev	11
G. F. Lawson, c Srikkanth, b Kapil Dev	6
R. M. Hogg, not out	2
Extras (1 b, 14 lb, 8 w, 2 nb)	25
60 overs. Total (9 wickets)	320

Fall of wickets: 1-11; 2-155; 3-159; 4-206; 5-254 6-277; 7-289; 8-301; 9-307.
Bowling: Kapil Dev 12-2-43-5; Sandhu 12-1-52-0; Binny 12-0-52-1; Shastri 2-0-16-0; Madan Lal 12-0-69-2; Patil 6-0-36-0; Amarnath 4-0-27-1.

INDIA

R. J. Shastri, lbw, b Lawson	11
K. Srikkanth, c Border, b Hogan	39
M. Amarnath, run out	2
D. B. Vengsarkar, lbw, b MacLeay	5
S. M. Patil, b MacLeay	0
Yashpal Sharma, c and b MacLeay	3
*Kapil Dev, b Hogan	40
Madan Lal, c Hogan, b MacLeay	27
R. M. Binny, lbw, b MacLeay	0
†S. M. H. Kirmani, b MacLeay	12
B. S. Sandhu, not out	9
Extras (1 b, 4 lb, 3 w, 2 nb)	10
37.5 overs. Total	158

Fall of wickets: 1-38; 2-43; 3-57; 4-57; 5-64; 6-66 7-124; 8-126; 9-136.
Bowling: Lawson 5-1-25-1; Hogg 7-2-23-0 Hogan 12-1-48-2; MacLeay 11.5-3-39-6; Border 2-0-13-0.

Umpires: D. O. Oslear and R. Palmer

Australia won by 162 runs
Man of the match: T. M. CHAPPELL

Steve Powell/All-Sport

Rain only threat to New Zealand

Sri Lanka, having run up two 280-plus totals, found the damp Bristol wicket and an in-form Richard Hadlee too much to cope with and went down to the most emphatic defeat of the three group matches they played in the south-west.

Hadlee won the Man of the Match award for his five for 25 in 10.1 overs, his performance being the best by a New Zealand bowler in the

when Hadlee came back for a deadly second spell.

New Zealand's worry was not so much whether they would win, but how soon. With clouds above, rain spattering in a strong wind and the experts forecasting rain at the end of the afternoon there was a need to hurry. Glenn Turner and John Wright did just that, and New Zealand reached tea at 120 for 3 off 25 overs, with 87 wanted.

Afterwards, with the threatened rain still not materialising, Howarth took over and, although he lost Jeffrey Crowe at 176 after they had put on 77 for the fourth wicket, the New Zealand skipper steered his side to the verge of victory. **RD**

Ian Newton

It's that man again! Richard Hadlee takes the catch to dismiss Kuruppu, in addition to his five wickets as a bowler.

competition. But it was an effective and economical spell by medium-pacer Ewen Chatfield that first succeeded in checking the batsmen.

It was left to captain Duleep Mendis again to bolster the batting, this time in a partnership of 71 in 20 overs with Madugalle each side of the lunch interval, but promise of acceleration was quickly stilled

SRI LANKA

S. Wettimuny, lbw, b Hadlee	7
B. Kuruppu, c Hadlee, b Chatfield	26
R. L. Dias, b Chatfield	25
*R. L. D. Mendis, b Hadlee	43
R. S. Madugalle, c Snedden, b Coney	60
A. Ranatunga, lbw, b Hadlee	0
D. S. de Silva, b Coney	13
†R. G. de Alwis, c Howarth, b Snedden	16
A. L. F. de Mel, c and b Hadlee	1
R. J. Ratnayake, b Hadlee	5
V. B. John, not out	2
Extras (6 lb, 1 w, 1 nb)	8
56.1 overs. Total	206

Fall of wickets: 1-16; 2-56; 3-73; 4-144; 5-144; 6-171; 7-196; 8-199; 9-199.
Bowling: Hadlee 10.1-4-25-5; Snedden 10-1-38-1; Chatfield 12-4-24-2; Cairns 7-0-35-0; Coney 12-0-44-2; M. D. Crowe 5-0-32-0.

NEW ZEALAND

G. M. Turner, c Mendis, b de Silva	50
J. G. Wright, lbw, b de Mel	45
*G. P. Howarth, c Madugalle, b Ratnayake	76
M. D. Crowe, c de Alwis, b de Mel	0
J. J. Crowe, lbw, b John	23
J. V. Coney, not out	2
†I. D. S. Smith, not out	4
Extras (6 lb, 3 w)	9
39.2 overs. Total (5 wickets)	209

Did not bat: R. J. Hadlee, B. L. Cairns, M. C. Snedden, E. J. Chatfield.
Fall of wickets: 1-89; 2-99; 3-110; 4-176; 5-205.
Bowling: de Mel 8-2-30-2; John 8.2-0-49-1; Ratnayake 12-0-60-1; de Silva 9-0-39-1; Ranatunga 2-0-22-0.

Umpires: H. D. Bird and D. R. Shepherd
New Zealand won by 5 wickets
Man of the match: R. J. HADLEE

How they stood

The third set of group matches had gone more or less according to the form-book, and now the question was whether the sides were settling down to their expected levels. Or were there more shocks ahead, like Zimbabwe's defeat of Australia or India's win over the mighty West Indies?

Zimbabwe had gained many friends in group B, but the West Indies, even without a major contribution yet from Viv Richards, were looking ominously strong. Australia's defeat of India suggested that they could take their place in

GROUP A	P	W	L	Pts	Runs/over
England	3	3	0	12	5·00
New Zealand	3	2	1	8	4·19
Pakistan	3	1	2	4	4·09
Sri Lanka	3	0	3	0	4·48

GROUP B	P	W	L	Pts	Runs/over
West Indies	3	2	1	8	4·29
India	3	2	1	8	3·82
Australia	3	1	2	4	4·63
Zimbabwe	3	1	2	4	3·56

the semi-finals (perhaps on faster scoring-rate) if they could put initial setbacks behind them. India were showing signs of fading after their dream start.

In group A, England were unrecognisable from the outfit which had retreated in some disorder from the Antipodes. Pakistan missed Imran Khan's bowling and showed their old fatal tendency to fall apart in adversity. New Zealand impressed as a team, while Sri Lanka had not enjoyed the luck which any outsiders need.

Whatever the outcome, the competition had by now caught the imagination of the country, by action and scenes like those shown on the following page.

NEW ZEALAND

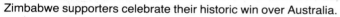

Zimbabwe supporters celebrate their historic win over Australia.

Above right: Mohsin Khan loses his helmet to a Willis bouncer.

Right: Every side was followed round the country by a band of committed supporters.

Left: Umpire Mervyn Kitchen is unimpressed by Dennis Lillee's frantic appeal against Zimbabwe's Fletcher.

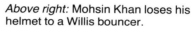

The great Sir Gary Sobers seems disappointed by his Sri Lankan protegés.

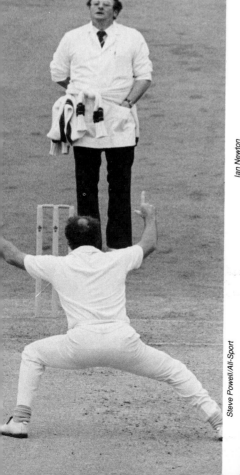

Ghosts of winter haunt England despite Gower's brilliance

The most exciting finish of the opening 14 World Cup matches ended with New Zealand claiming a two-wicket victory over England at Edgbaston with just one ball to spare.

The home batting, apart from the elegant David Gower and purposeful Graeme Fowler, was at times reckless – in fact, shades of winter disasters. Yet England's innings, after Bob Willis had won the toss for the third time in four matches, was given a confident start by Graeme

Fowler and Chris Tavare as 63 was posted on the scoreboard inside 19 overs.

Howarth quickly shelved his main strike bowlers, Richard Hadlee and Lance Cairns, seeing that the wicket was unlikely to help them break through. In their place the gentle Jeremy Coney and spinner John Bracewell attempted to contain the home side and got through their overs at such a rate that 20 were delivered in the first 60 minutes – a rare achievement in a decade dominated by pacemen off endless runs.

Facing them was Fowler, who looked extremely confident in making 69, and Ian Botham, batting at no. 3 after Willis changed his order for the first time in the series in the hope that the all-rounder would take the slow bowlers apart. Willis's disruption was a failure. Botham failed to take his opportunity of a long innings trying to hit the ball before his eye was in. One six sailed high over long leg but on 12 he fell to a stinging return catch by Bracewell.

Trump card

Howarth's move was to prove a trump card, as Hadlee and Cairns returned to the action later to claim three wickets each. Only Gower, taking his aggregate to 309 from four World Cup innings at an average of over 100, played with any sense of responsibility. Sadly, he ran out of partners when only eight short of his second century of the competition and his fourth against New Zealand inside six months.

Steadying partners

Willis, cheered on by his home crowd, removed Glenn Turner and Bruce Edgar in his first nine deliveries with only three runs scored. But Howarth, despite being weakened by a 48-hour attack of dysentery, found steadying partners in the two Crowe brothers and the score was 75 before the fourth wicket went down in the 27th over.

Success for Allott at last as he bowls Jeff Crowe.

The tide turned in a partnership of 71 between Howarth and Coney that only ended when the Kiwi leader attempted a second run against Graham Dilley's powerful throw from long leg.

New Zealand entered the last over from Paul Allott needing just four more and, when wicket-keeper Ian Gould let the second ball through for two byes, New Zealand knew four points were in the bag to take them level with England at the top of the Group A table. **GO**

ENGLAND

G. Fowler, c J. J. Crowe, b Chatfield	69
C. J. Tavare, c Cairns, b Coney	18
I. T. Botham, c and b Bracewell	12
D. I. Gower, not out	92
A. J. Lamb, c J. J. Crowe, b Cairns	8
M. W. Gatting, b Cairns	1
†I. J. Gould, lbw, b Cairns	4
V. J. Marks, b Hadlee	5
G. R. Dilley, b Hadlee	10
P. J. W. Allott, c Smith, b Hadlee	0
*R. G. D. Willis, lbw, b Chatfield	0
Extras (4 b, 10 lb, 1 w)	15

55.2 overs. Total 234

Fall of wickets: 1-63; 2-77; 3-117; 4-143; 5-154; 6-162; 7-203; 8-233; 9-233.
Bowling: Hadlee 10-3-32-3; Cairns 11-0-44-3; Coney 12-2-27-1; Bracewell 12-0-66-1; Chatfield 10.2-0-50-2.

NEW ZEALAND

G. T. Turner, lbw, b Willis	2
B. A. Edgar, c Gould, b Willis	1
*G. P. Howarth, run out	60
J. J. Crowe, b Allott	17
M. D. Crowe, b Marks	20
J. V. Coney, not out	66
†I. D. S. Smith, b Botham	4
R. J. Hadlee, b Willis	31
R. L. Cairns, lbw, b Willis	5
J. G. Bracewell, not out	4
Extras (2 b, 22 lb, 1 w, 3 nb)	28

59.5 overs. Total (8 wickets) 238

Did not bat: E. J. Chatfield.
Fall of wickets: 1-2; 2-3; 3-47; 4-75; 5-146; 6-151; 7-221; 8-231.
Bowling: Willis 12-1-42-4; Dilley 12-1-43-0; Botham 12-1-47-1; Allott 11.5-2-44-1; Marks 12-1-34-1.

Umpires: K. E. Palmer and J. Birkenshaw
New Zealand won by 2 wickets
Man of the match: J. V. CONEY

Steve Powell/All-Sport

Richards plays himself back into form

Viv Richards, out of touch after three low scores, chose this match to demonstrate to his army of devoted West Indian followers that he was moving up the gears in preparation for the team's surge towards another World Cup Final. If it was not a vintage Richards century, none of his exuberant compatriots in the 12,000 crowd enjoying a day of unbroken sunshine was going to complain.

This revenge win – in answer to India's surprise 34-run success at Old Trafford the previous Thursday – was however marred to some extent by an injury to Dilip Vengsarkar, the no. 4 Indian batsman, who was struck under the jaw by a short-pitched delivery which reared sharply. He had made a valuable 32

in a partnership of 68 with Mohinder Amarnath.

Amarnath eventually went at 193 for a gallant 80, but only the captain, Kapil Dev, with 36 offered further resistance as Michael Holding came back with two wickets to finish with 3 for 40. The last five wickets went down for just 23.

Steady partnership
The West Indies innings had been dominated by Richards who, when he first arrived in the fifth over after Greenidge had been taken at slip off Kapil Dev, hardly looked likely to add to his 40 runs from three previous innings. But after a shaky start he gradually began to blossom in a steady partnership with Des Haynes, also trying to find some form.

When Haynes was out, Lloyd was really getting into his stride, having swung Binny over mid-wicket for six, when a misunderstanding with Richards left him stranded and wicket-keeper Kirmani ran him out with a throw that hit the stumps direct.

From 198 for 3 in the forty-fifth over when Lloyd was out, the West Indies lost wickets steadily. Richards was sixth out at 240, having hit six fours as well as a gigantic six to the pavilion roof. He was taken behind the wicket when Sandhu found an edge after Richards had batted 202 minutes, receiving 146 balls.

Gomes kept the runs ticking over near the end with a chirpy 27 not out, but only 59 came from the final ten overs as the total reached a substantial but not insuperable 282 for 9. Binny finished best of the Indian bowlers. **RD**

Vengsarkar was steadying the Indian ship but took no further part in the match after receiving a blow from Marshall.

WEST INDIES

C. G. Greenidge, c Vengsarkar, b Kapil Dev .	9
D. L. Haynes, c Kapil Dev, b Amarnath	38
I. V. A. Richards, c Kirmani, b Sandhu	119
*C. H. Lloyd, run out	41
S. F. A. Bacchus, b Binny	8
†P. J. Dujon, c Shastri, b Binny	9
H. A. Gomes, not out	27
A. M. E. Roberts, c Patil, b Binny	7
M. D. Marshall, run out	4
M. A. Holding, c sub, b Madan Lal	2
W. W. Davis, not out	2
Extras (13 lb, 5 w)	18
60 overs. Total (9 wickets)	282

Fall of wickets: 1-17; 2-118; 3-198; 4-213; 5-239; 6-240; 7-257; 8-270; 9-280.
Bowling: Kapil Dev 12-0-46-1; Sandhu 12-2-42-1; Binny 12-0-71-3; Amarnath 12-0-58-1; Madan Lal 12-0-47-1.

INDIA

K. Srikkanth, c Dujon, b Roberts	2
R. Shastri, c Dujon, b Roberts	6
M. Amarnath, c Lloyd, b Holding	80
D. B. Vengsarkar, retired hurt	32
S. M. Patil, c and b Gomes	21
Yashpal Sharma, run out	9
*Kapil Dev, c Haynes, b Holding	36
R. M. H. Binny, lbw, b Holding	1
Madan Lal, not out	8
†S. M. H. Kirmani, b Marshall	0
B. S. Sandhu, run out	0
Extras (3 b, 13 lb, 5 nb)	21
53.1 overs. Total	216

Fall of wickets: 1-2; 2-21; 3-130; 4-143; 5-193; 6-195; 7-212; 8-214; 9-216.
Bowling: Roberts 9-1-29-2; Holding 9.1-0-40-3; Marshall 11-3-20-1; Davis 12-2-51-0; Gomes 12-1-55-1.

Umpires: B. J. Meyer and D. R. Shepherd.
West Indies won by 66 runs
Man of the match: I. V. A. RICHARDS

Adrian Murrell/All-Sport

Australia safely home after Zimbabwe threaten double

Dave Cannon/All-Sport

Australia finally overcame the indomitable spirit of the Zimbabweans and gained some sort of revenge for their defeat earlier in the competition, but not before they had been given an uncomfortable run for their money.

The underdogs lost off the penultimate ball of the match, but the size of the Australian victory concealed the compelling nature of the battle, which until the last eight overs could have gone either way.

Zimbabwe needed 61 from just over eight overs with five wickets remaining in reply to Australia's 272 for 7. At this stage, in gathering gloom and with the 4000 crowd behind them, Zimbabwe were handily placed to complete a humiliating double over their illustrious opponents.

David Houghton and Kevin Curran had added 103 runs for the sixth wicket with ominous assurance when Trevor Chappell and Rodney Hogg swung the match irrevocably towards the Australians with a cool and vital spell of bowling. Chappell's medium-pace guile trapped Curran with the score at 212 and Zimbabwean hopes died with his dismissal. Ian Butchart and Peter Rawson were leg before to successive deliveries in the next over from Hogg and, when the despairing Houghton finally lifted Chappell to short mid-off, Zimbabwe had lost four wickets for one run in eight balls.

It was particularly harsh on Houghton, the wicket-keeper, who hit a six off Chappell and eight fours during his 110-minute innings, but once he had gone there was never any chance of a recovery. John

Traicos and Vincent Hogg narrowed the margin of defeat with a brave last-wicket stand of 27 but it was all an anti-climax.

Australia had made steady progress after deciding to bat first on a flat and easy-paced wicket. Graeme Wood, restored after injury, might have been run out for 16 but survived to top-score with 73.

The departure of Wood in the second over after lunch and the potentially belligerent David Hookes at 150 halted Australia's burgeoning progress. It needed the

AUSTRALIA

G. W. Wood, c Rawson, b Traicos	73
T. M. Chappell, c Traicos, b Rawson	22
*K. J. Hughes, b Traicos	31
D. W. Hookes, c Brown, b Fletcher	10
G. N. Yallop, c Houghton, b Curran	20
A. R. Border, b Butchart	43
†R. W. Marsh, not out	35
K. H. MacLeay, c Rawson, b Butchart	9
T. G. Hogan, not out	5
Extras (16 lb, 2 w, 6 nb)	24
60 overs. Total (7 wickets)	272

Did not bat: D. K. Lillee, R. M. Hogg.
Fall of wickets: 1-46; 2-124; 3-150; 4-150; 5-219; 6-231; 7-249.
Bowling: Hogg 9-2-34-0; Rawson 9-0-50-1; Fletcher 9-1-27-1; Butchart 10-0-52-2; Traicos 12-1-28-2; Curran 11-0-57-1.

ZIMBABWE

R. B. Brown, c Marsh, b Hogan	38
G. A. Paterson, lbw, b Hogg	17
J. G. Heron, run out	3
A. J. Pycroft, run out	13
†D. L. Houghton, c Hughes, b Chappell	84
*D. A. G. Fletcher, b Hogan	2
K. M. Curran, lbw, b Chappell	35
I. Butchart, lbw, b Hogg	0
P. W. E. Rawson, lbw, b Hogg	0
A. J. Traicos, b Chappell	19
V. R. Hogg, not out	7
Extras (1 b, 10 lb, 1 w, 10 nb)	22
59.5 overs. Total	240

Fall of wickets: 1-48; 2-53; 3-79; 4-97; 5-109; 6-212; 7-213; 8-213; 9-213.
Bowling: Hogg 12-0-40-3; Lillee 9-1-23-0; Hogan 12-0-33-2; MacLeay 9-0-45-0; Border 9-1-30-0; Chappell 8.5-0-47-3.

Umpires: D. G. L. Evans and R. Palmer
Australia won by 32 runs
Man of the match: D. L. HOUGHTON

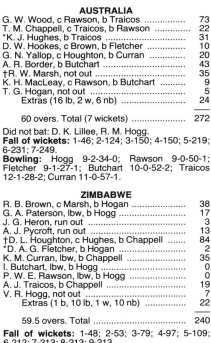
The umpire agreed with Rodney Hogg that Grant Paterson was plumb in front.

steadying influence of Graham Yallop and Allan Border to repair the damage.

Aggressive hitting

Houghton, later to be named Man of the Match by Roy Marshall, removed Yallop with a leg-side catch but the stage was set, even after Border's dismissal, for some aggressive hitting by Rodney Marsh and Ken MacLeay. Marsh, just the man for the situation, struck Butchart and Curran for sixes and MacLeay straight-drove another from Butchart.

Even when Robin Brown, the dominant partner in a first-wicket stand of 48 with Grant Paterson, was out to the last ball before tea with the score at 79, Andrew Pycroft, Zimbabwe's principal batsman, was in control and an interesting finish looked in prospect. But in going for a sharp single, Pycroft was brilliantly run out by Marsh's throw to the bowler's end.

Tom Hogan's flat left-arm spin accounted for Duncan Fletcher and Zimbabwe were 109 for 5. Then came the Houghton-Curran stand and it looked as if Zimbabwe might win before the final twists of a fascinating duel. **PS**

Qadir bamboozles Sri Lankans after Imran stops rot

Sri Lanka arrived at Headingley to find the classic conditions of an overcast day with the sun hiding behind the clouds. They won the toss and put Pakistan in to bat. De Mel, with a high action and good technique, maintained the perfect length and his outswing proved too tempting for Mohsin Khan, Mansoor Akhtar and Zaheer. Pakistan were groggy at 43 for 5, and de Mel retired from the attack with a first spell of 8-1-13-3.

Sri Lanka could not believe it was happening and, instead of pressing home the considerable advantage, took the opportunity to introduce lesser bowlers. It was an expensive change of policy and two dropped catches also proved further dear misses as Shahid Mahboob and Imran Khan produced a World Cup record sixth-wicket stand of 144 in 36 overs.

Far from daunting

As the humidity lessened, the potency of the attack evaporated and batting become simpler. But de Mel returned to stamp his authority on the innings. Imran just had time to register the first century in the World Cup by a Pakistani batsman before the innings closed at 235 for 7.

This looked a far from daunting target when Sidath Wettimuny and Roy Dias were together. Dias drove beautifully at anything remotely up to him and, with his partner content to applaud his efforts, Sri Lanka moved smoothly into complete control. With half their innings left, 13 were wanted with nine wickets in hand.

Inexplicable panic

But Dias, beaten off the pitch by Qadir as he moved for another drive, started an inexplicable panic in the dressing room that spilled over onto the pitch. When they should have been conserving wickets for the final victory push, Sri Lanka had rush of blood against leg-spinner Qadir and lost four wickets in three overs. Qadir's haul was three in eight deliveries, while only four runs were added. De Silva, run out by a throw from mid-wicket, and wicket keeper de Alwis, taken at slip, added to the panic.

Sri Lanka had virtually snatched defeat from the jaws of victory, but they showed an indomitable spirit and willingness to battle through their mistakes, personified in a last wicket partnership that brought the match back within their grasp. It was finally snatched away by Imran holding de Mel at deep mid-off with nine balls to spare and Sri Lanka 11 runs away from a victory that would have effectively ended Pakistan's challenge.

DF

PAKISTAN

Mohsin Khan, c Ranatunga, b de Mel	3
Mansoor Akhtar, c de Alwis, b de Mel	6
Zaheer Abbas, c Dias, b de Mel	15
Javed Miandad, lbw, b Ratnayake	7
*Imran Khan, not out	102
Ijaz Fakih, lbw, b Ratnayake	0
Shahid Mahboob, c de Silva, b de Mel	77
Sarfraz Nawaz, c Madugalle, b de Mel	9
Abdul Qadir, not out	5
Extras (1 b, 4 lb, 4 w, 2 nb)	11
60 overs. Total (7 wickets)	**235**

Did not bat: †Wasim Bari, Rashid Khan.
Fall of wickets: 1-6; 2-25; 3-30; 4-43; 5-43; 6-187; 7-204.
Bowling: de Mel 12-1-39-5; John 12-1-48-0; Ratnayake 12-2-42-2; Ranatunga 11-0-49-0; de Silva 12-1-42-0; Wettimuny 1-0-4-0.

SRI LANKA

S. Wettimuny, c Shahid, b Rashid	50
B. Kuruppu, b Rashid	12
R. L. Dias, st Wasim Bari, b Qadir	47
*R. L. Mendis, c Wasim Bari, b Qadir	33
R. J. Ratnayake, st Wasim Bari, b Qadir	1
R. S. Madugalle, c Qadir, b Shahid	26
A. Ranatunga, c Zaheer, b Qadir	0
D. S. de Silva, run out	1
†R. G. de Alwis, c Miandad, b Qadir	4
A. L. F. de Mel, c Imran, b Sarfraz	17
V. B. John, not out	6
Extras (8 lb, 17 w, 2 nb)	27
58.3 overs. Total	**224**

Fall of wickets: 1-22; 2-101; 3-162; 4-162; 5-166; 6-166; 7-171; 8-193; 9-199.
Bowling: Rashid 12-4-31-2; Sarfraz 11.3-2-25-1; Shahid 10-1-62-1; Mansoor 1-0-8-0; Ijaz 12-0-27-0; Qadir 12-1-44-5.

Umpires: D. O. Oslear and A. G. T. Whitehead

Pakistan won by 11 runs

Man of the match: ABDUL QADIR

Mohsin Khan watches in horror as he edges de Mel straight into Ranatunga's waiting hands.

Kapil Dev shatters record and Zimbabwean hopes

The lovely cricket ground at Tunbridge Wells seems an improbable setting for a meeting between India and Zimbabwe, yet it quickly absorbed them, bestowing on them some form of honorary membership for the day.

When the fixture list was first drawn up, the game seemed to have little significance. Here, one thought, would be a meeting of the two minnows of Group B. By 18th June, West Indies and Australia would be assured of a place in the semi-final, but then Australia had fallen to Zimbabwe, and India had beaten West Indies, and so both teams arrived at Tunbridge Wells with much to play for.

The mighty Gavaskar, badly out of form, had been dropped from the previous game and owed his recall to Vengsarkar's injury. It was an unhappy return. Rawson's first ball lifted sharply and uncomfortably at him to cast immediate doubts about the wicket, and the doubts were confirmed on the last ball of that opening over when Gavaskar aimed simply to leg and was lbw.

Kapil Dev hits out during his stunning 175 not out.

Trevor Jones/All-Sport

For India, there was worse to follow. They did not score a run until the third over and, in the fifth, Amarnath edged Rawson to wicket-keeper Houghton, although the batsman showed a reluctance to leave. Srikkanth lifted Curran high to mid-off, where Butchart took a splendid running catch.

Patil and Yashpal Sharma showed little signs of confidence. Patil was caught behind on the leg-side and Yashpal Sharma also fell to the wicket-keeper. In the thirteenth over, India were 17 for 5.

One of the very great innings

Kapil Dev, however, mixed sound defence with a willingness to punish the loose ball. He raised the hundred and his own 50 in the thirty-sixth over but, lunching at 106 for 7, the Indians could not have been happy.

There was an immediate air of determination after lunch. Dev and Madan Lal added 69 in 16 overs, until Madan Lal became Houghton's fourth victim.

This was in effect Zimbabwe's last piece of joy. Kirmani bristled confidence and Kapil Dev hit strongly all round the ground. Suddenly, the crowd was aware that they were watching one of the very great innings. He had come in at 9 for 4 in the tenth over, and he reached his 100 in the forty-ninth over. The century partnership came in 13 overs of brilliant batting, and Zimbabwe's fielding so good early on, wilted. The innings closed on 266, with Kapil Dev, six sixes and 16 fours, on 175 not out, the highest score ever made in a one-day international.

Stupid run-out

Zimbabwe began briskly enough, but Paterson and Heron fell in successive overs and Pycroft left at 61. Brown was stupidly run out, and Fletcher fell to a marvellous catch on the boundary.

Kevin Curran then played a glorious innings of 73. At the end of the fifty-fifth over, Zimbabwe were 226 for 8, only two runs short of India at the same point, but Curran played a weak, uncharacteristic shot and was taken at mid-off, and India and Kapil Dev took the honours. **DL**

INDIA	
S. M. Gavaskar, lbw, b Rawson	0
K. Srikkanth, c Butchart, b Curran	0
M. Amarnath, c Houghton, b Rawson	5
S. M. Patil, c Houghton, b Curran	1
Yashpal Sharma, c Houghton, b Rawson	9
Kapil Dev, not out	175
R. M. H. Binny, lbw, b Traicos	22
R. J. Shastri, c Pycroft, b Fletcher	1
Madan Lal, c Houghton, b Curran	17
†S. M. H. Kirmani, not out	24
Extras (9 lb, 3 w)	12
60 overs. Total (8 wickets)	266

Did not bat: B. S. Sandhu.
Fall of wickets: 1-0; 2-6; 3-6; 4-9; 5-17; 6-77; 7-78; 8-140.
Bowling: Rawson 12-4-47-3; Curran 12-1-65-3; Butchart 12-2-38-0; Fletcher 12-2-59-1; Traicos 2-0-45-1.

ZIMBABWE	
R. D. Brown, run out	35
G. A. Paterson, lbw, b Binny	23
J. G. Heron, run out	3
A. J. Pycroft, c Kirmani, b Sandhu	6
†D. L. Houghton, lbw, b Madan Lal	17
*D. A. G. Fletcher, c Kapil Dev, b Amarnath	13
K. M. Curran, c Shastri, b Madan Lal	73
I. Butchart, b Binny	18
G. E. Peckover, c Yashpal, b Madan Lal	14
P. W. E. Rawson, not out	2
A. J. Traicos, c and b Kapil Dev	3
Extras (17 lb, 7 w, 4 nb)	28
57 overs. Total	235

Fall of wickets: 1-44; 2-48; 3-61; 4-86; 5-103; 6-113; 7-168; 8-189; 9-230.
Bowling: Kapil Dev 11-1-32-1; Sandhu 11-2-44-1; Binny 11-2-45-2; Madan Lal 11-2-42-3; Amarnath 12-1-37-1; Shastri 1-0-7-0.

Umpires: M. J. Kitchen and B. J. Meyer
India won by 31 runs　　**Man of the match: KAPIL DEV**

West Indies give Hughes's men a lesson in pacing an innings

With a full house of 25,000 enjoying a day of glorious sunshine and some high-quality batting as 549 runs were scored, this was an occasion that had all the atmosphere worthy of the Final itself.

In what the West Indies clearly saw as a dress rehearsal for the real thing the following Saturday, there were some notable performances, particularly from the imperious Viv Richards whose Man of the Match winning performance, his second in a row, deserved a century, but in fact left him five runs short. There were some marvellous contributions too from Australia's Kim Hughes, Graham Yallop, David Hookes and Rodney Marsh, and from the West Indies opener, Gordon Greenidge.

Luck looked to be on Hughes's side when he won the toss for a fifth consecutive World Cup game and sensibly took use of a firm, dry pitch.

David Hookes after taking a swing at Larry Gomes and missing. The injured Hughes watches from square leg.

Adrian Murrell/All-Sport

Australia hoped to build a match-winning total to avoid having to go to Chelmsford on the Monday needing to beat India to qualify for the semi-final.

Hughes lamed

Marshall dismissed both openers for 37 in a lively five-over spell for 17 runs before Hughes and Hookes joined in a recovery stand of 101 in 26 overs. It was far from easy for Hughes, who pulled a thigh muscle in the ninth over going for over-throws, and for the remainder of the 36 overs he batted he needed the assistance of a runner.

When Hookes went at 138 and Hughes followed at 176, for a while the Australian innings went into the doldrums – only 40 runs came from 10 overs up to the 50-over mark. Marsh and Yallop, the latter aided by two bad catching lapses by Marshall and Haynes, led the final 10-over flourish that produced 77 runs.

Marsh hit 37, with two sixes and a four off successive deliveries from Holding in a 26-ball whirlwind knock, and Yallop finished unbeaten on 52. Marshall was easily the best of the bowlers with 2 for 36.

Masterly Richards

The West Indies innings was a triumph of paced effort, with the batsmen showing the sometimes more frenetic Australians just how to go about selecting the right balls to hit. Greenidge and Haynes were never in the slightest difficulty as they added 79 in 18 overs before Haynes dragged a ball from left-arm

spinner Tom Hogan onto his stumps and was bowled for 33. Then came Richards and for the next 27 overs the Australian attack, with the exception of the steady Rodney Hogg, was despatched to all parts and 124 runs were raised. Richards, following up his 119 against India at the Oval, was at his most masterly, stroking the ball with arrogant ease and producing shots that only he could play. He hit three superb sixes, two over long-on off Hogan and Chappell and the best of them over extra cover off Thomson.

Greenidge was caught off Hogg for 90, made in 185 minutes with eight fours, and when Gomes was bowled by Chappell in the fifty-third over after making 15, another 36 were needed with Richards 23 short of his 100. Clive Lloyd did his best to help his partner to three figures, but when it became an impossibility, finished proceedings himself with a lofted shot for four, with 13 balls of the innings left. Richards made his 95 off 117 balls and had nine fours as well as three sixes. **RD**

AUSTRALIA

G. M. Wood, b Marshall	1?
T. M. Chappell, c Dujon, b Marshall	5
*K. J. Hughes, b Gomes	69
D. W. Hookes, c Greenidge, b Davis	56
G. N. Yallop, not out	52
A. R. Border, c and b Gomes	11
†R. W. Marsh, c Haynes, b Holding	37
T. G. Hogan, not out	0
Extras (1 b, 18 lb, 6 w, 1 nb)	2?
60 overs. Total (6 wickets)	27?

Did not bat: J. R. Thomson, D. K. Lillee, R. M. Hogg
Fall of wickets: 1-10; 2-37; 3-138; 4-176; 5-202 6-266.
Bowling: Roberts 12-0-51-0; Marshall 12-0-36-2 Davis 12-0-57-1; Holding 12-1-56-1; Gomes 12-0-47-2.

WEST INDIES

C. G. Greenidge, c Hughes, b Hogg	90
D. L. Haynes, b Hogan	33
I. V. A. Richards, not out	95
H. A. Gomes, b Chappell	15
*C. H. Lloyd, not out	19
Extras (3 b, 18 lb, 1 w, 2 nb)	24
57.5 overs. Total (3 wickets)	27?

Did not bat: S. F. A. Bacchus, †P. J. Dujon M. D. Marshall, A. M. E. Roberts, M. A. Holding, W. W. Davis.
Fall of wickets: 1-79; 2-203; 3-238.
Bowling: Hogg 12-0-25-1; Thomson 11-0-64-0 Hogan 12-0-60-1; Lillee 12-0-52-0; Chappell 10.5-0-51-1.

Umpires: K. E. Palmer and A. G. T. Whitehead
West Indies won by 7 wickets
Man of the match: I. V. A. RICHARDS

Surprise defeat puts NZ under pressure for place in last four

Sri Lanka, without a point in four previous matches, re-affirmed their right to keep company with the major cricketing nations with a surprising but thoroughly merited three-wicket victory over New Zealand. New Zealand would now have to beat Pakistan in their last group match to go on to the semi-finals.

With hazy sunshine and the Derby pitch tinged with green, the toss was crucial and Sri Lanka took full advantage of winning it to reduce New Zealand to 47 for 4, then 116 for 9, the brisk medium pace of de Mel

earning him 5 for 32 to better his 5 for 39 against Pakistan two days earlier.

This was the best-ever bowling by a Sri Lankan in the World Cup and enough to earn him the Man of the Match award from adjudicator David Allen, the former England off-spinner, but hardly less vital was the contribution of de Silva. The leg-spinner took 2 for 11 in 12 overs of sustained control and intelligent variation to tighten the screw on the

the appropriate blend of watchfulness and aggression, the last-wicket pair suffering few alarms against Sri Lanka's second-line bowling.

Enterprising late flourish

De Mel's fine throw from mid-on ended the resistance, Snedden failing to get home for a second run, but the enterprise of this late flourish at least demanded of Sri Lanka a scoring rate above three runs an over.

Kuruppu had few moments of insecurity in reaching 50 in 32 overs as the seamers toiled in conditions now considerably less encouraging than they had been in the morning. He had hit ten fours before driving a fierce return catch to Snedden, a dismissal which set off a nervous spell in which Mendis, Madugalle and

NEW ZEALAND

. M. Turner, c Dias, b de Mel	6
. G. Wright, c de Alwis, b de Mel	0
G. P. Howarth, b Ratnayake	15
. D. Crowe, lbw, b Ratnayake	8
. A. Edgar, c Samarasekera, b de Silva	27
V. Coney, c sub, b de Silva	22
. J. Hadlee, c Madugalle, b de Mel	15
W. K. Lees, c Ranatunga, b de Mel	2
. L. Cairns, c Dias, b de Mel	6
. C. Snedden, run out	40
. J. Chatfield, not out	19
Extras (4 b, 5 lb, 11 w, 1 nb)	21
58.2 overs. Total	181

Fall of wickets: 1-8; 2-8; 3-32; 4-47; 5-88; 6-91; 7-105; 8-115; 9-116.

Bowling: de Mel 12-4-32-5; Ratnayake 11-4-18-2; Ranatunga 10-2-50-0; de Silva 12-5-11-2; Samarasekera 11.2-2-38-0; Wettimuny 2-0-11-0.

SRI LANKA

. Wettimuny, b Cairns	4
. Kuruppu, c and b Snedden	62
. Ranatunga, b Crowe	15
. L. Dias, not out	64
. R. D. Mendis, lbw, b Chatfield	0
. S. Madugalle, c Lees, b Snedden	6
. A. R. Samarasekera, c Lees, b Hadlee	5
. S. de Silva, run out	2
R. G. de Alwis, not out	11
Extras (1 b, 4 lb, 10 w)	15
52.5 overs. Total (7 wickets)	184

Did not bat: A. L. F. de Mel, R. J. Ratnayake.

Fall of wickets: 1-15; 2-49; 3-129; 4-130; 5-139; 6-151; 7-161.

Bowling: Hadlee 12-3-16-1; Cairns 10-2-35-1; Snedden 10.5-1-58-2; Chatfield 12-3-23-1; Crowe 2-2-15-1; Coney 4-1-22-0.

Umpires: D. J. Constant and B. Leadbeater

Sri Lanka won by 3 wickets

Man of the match: A. L. F. DE MEL

A disconsolate Coney sets off for the pavilion while Samarasekera congratulates substitute fielder Fernando.

middle order after de Mel, finding generous movement through the air, had removed New Zealand's two most highly regarded batsmen, Turner and Wright, with consecutive balls in his second over. Turner misjudged de Mel's away-swing and Wright, on home territory, perished to a casual stroke.

Only when Snedden and Chatfield came together did New Zealand find

Samarasekera all succumbed to vague defensive strokes and the Sri Lanka run-rate dwindled.

But Dias's discreet aggression saw Sri Lanka home with something to spare, rewarding them and their hundreds of fans for bringing a splash of colour and a carnival atmosphere to what is normally regarded as one of the county circuit's bleakest venues. **NH**

33

Only Miandad shines as Pakistan fold up

Watching Pakistan without Imran's bowling was an irresistible reminder of one of the most beloved clichés in all English: Hamlet without the Prince. With less than one-half of the great all-rounder's game functioning, Pakistani spirits burned low. The many talents around him, instead of trying to redress the balance by raising their own performances, appeared to decline with him. Pakistan were a shadow of the side that had smashed England at Lord's in 1982.

On a slow but easy-paced wicket on which the only slight difficulty was the odd low bounce, the outfield being very fast, Pakistan's 232 for 8 was an abject performance. Willis and Dilley made a fast and hostile England opening attack and had not Dilley suffered a slight strain at the top of his right thigh in his third over, we might have seen him fully regain his place as the premier English prospect. The delivery that removed Zaheer for 0, a body blow to the innings, was 24-carat.

There were ample opportunities for Pakistan to prosper against a mundane Botham, a defensive Allott and an all-too-obviously tempting Marks, but very few were taken. Miandad alone lived up to his reputation, contemptuously despatching anything below first class and turning Marks's more obvious enticements into runs.

Botham, having contributed very little, virtually ended the contest when, 25 yards out and somewhere between deep gully and short third man, he ran out Miandad with a pounce and throw of such speed and accuracy that what should have been a comfortable run became a disaster. As swift and as accurate was umpire Oslear's decision.

Man of the Match

England spent 57.2 overs knocking off the runs, the 20,000-plus crowd refusing to budge until they had received every penny worth of value for the £83,000 they had subscribed. In truth, they got short change. Fowler's 69 was his third World Cup half-century and as a Lancastrian at Old Trafford with Roy Tattersall the adjudicator, he had to be Man of the Match although Miandad's innings was of a much higher class.

England's other batsmen did their duty, trying hard not to appear bored, while much of the Pakistan bowling might have provoked court-martial in Lahore. **D**

PAKISTAN

Mohsin Khan, c Marks, b Allott	32
Mudassar Nazar, c Gould, b Dilley	18
Zaheer Abbas, c Gould, b Dilley	0
Javed Miandad, run out	67
*Imran Khan, c Willis, b Marks	13
Wasim Raja, c Willis, b Marks	15
Ijaz Fakih, not out	42
Sarfraz Nawaz, b Willis	17
Abdul Qadir, run out	6
†Wasim Bari, not out	2
Extras (3 b, 14 lb, 2 w, 1 nb)	20
60 overs. Total (8 wickets)	232

Did not bat: Rashid Khan.
Fall of wickets: 1-33; 2-34; 3-87; 4-116; 5-144; 6-169; 7-204; 8-221.
Bowling: Willis 12-3-37-1; Dilley 12-2-46-2; Allott 12-1-33-1; Botham 12-1-51-0; Marks 12-0-45-2.

ENGLAND

G. Fowler, c Miandad, b Mudassar	69
C. J. Tavare, c Wasim Raja, b Zaheer	58
D. I. Gower, c Zaheer, b Mudassar	31
A. J. Lamb, not out	38
M. W. Gatting, not out	14
Extras (1 b, 15 lb, 7 w)	23
57.2 overs. Total (3 wickets)	233

Did not bat: I. T. Botham, †I. J. Gould, V. J. Marks, G. R. Dilley, P. J. W. Allott, *R. G. D. Willis.
Fall of wickets: 1-115; 2-165; 3-181.
Bowling: Rashid 11-1-58-0; Sarfraz 10.2-2-22-0; Qadir 11-0-51-0; Ijaz 6-0-19-0; Mudassar 12-2-34-2; Zaheer 7-0-26-1.

Umpires: H. D. Bird and D. O. Oslear
England won by 7 wickets
Man of the match: G. FOWLER

Dilley and Gould celebrate their joint effort in dismissing the dangerous Zaheer for a duck.

New Zealand out in last-over thriller

Pakistan won their final Group A qualifying match and so improbably scraped a semi-final place against West Indies at the Oval. The finish was a frantic one and typical of Pakistan's multi-talented team, who qualified despite doing most things wrong in the tournament.

After winning the toss, the Pakistan innings revolved round an unbroken stand of 147 in 18 overs by Zaheer who scored a lovely 103, and Imran whose 79 was full of powerful drives.

At tea New Zealand wanted 172 off 35 overs with Geoff Howarth looking well set against everyone except Qadir. In fact, Qadir confused all their main batsmen, who played him as though he was bowling hand grenades in a dense fog down the slow lane of the M1.

Inspirationally, Imran gave the ball to Zaheer, whose first ball (a chest-high full toss) was eagerly seized upon by Howarth. Not so eagerly, though, as Miandad seized the catch at square leg to complete the 'sucker dismissal' of the competition.

Martin Crowe played with increasing authority for his 43, but an across-the-line stroke to the persistent Mudassar, together with minimal contributions from big hitters Hadlee and Cairns, reduced New Zealand to 152 for 7.

Pakistan seemed in total control with 75 still needed off eight overs and only Bracewell and Chatfield to come. But one-day cricket seldom lets the lights go out in a game, and Bracewell turned the improbable into a realistic winning chance by hitting Sarfraz and Rashid to such good purpose that 53 came off five overs.

Hysterical anxiety

With three overs to go, 22 were needed and Pakistan were in tatters, with the large contingent of their supporters in the 5000 crowd beside themselves with hysterical anxiety.

Six runs came off the first five deliveries in the fifty-eighth over, but the final ball of that over settled the match when Bracewell all but hooked Sarfraz for six, only to see Mohsin catch him a few yards inside the boundary.

A typical one-day run-out of Coney for 51 off the first ball of the last over brought the match to an end amid scenes which reflected no credit to the Trent Bridge ground authorities, umpire David Evans being hustled and floored as he tried to reach the pavilion.   **JB**

Vasim Bari breaks the wicket, Coney is run out and Pakistan are through to the semi-finals.

Dave Cannon/All-Sport

PAKISTAN

Mohsin Khan, c Cairns, b Coney	33
Mudassar Nazar, b Coney	15
Javed Miandad, b Hadlee	25
Zaheer Abbas, not out	103
*Imran Khan, not out	79
Extras (1 b, 2 lb, 2 w, 1 nb)	6
60 overs. Total (3 wickets)	261

Did not bat: Ijaz Fakih, Shahid Mahboob, Sarfraz Nawaz, Abdul Qadir, †Wasim Bari, Rashid Khan.
Fall of wickets: 1-48; 2-54; 3-114.
Bowling: Hadlee 12-1-61-1; Cairns 12-1-45-0; Chatfield 12-0-57-0; Coney 12-0-42-2; Bracewell 12-0-50-0.

NEW ZEALAND

G. M. Turner, c Wasim Bari, b Sarfraz	4
J. G. Wright, c Imran, b Qadir	19
*G. P. Howarth, c Miandad, b Zaheer	39
M. D. Crowe, b Mudassar	43
B. A. Edgar, lbw, b Shahid	6
J. V. Coney, run out	51
R. J. Hadlee, c Mohsin, b Mudassar	11
B. L. Cairns, c Imran, b Qadir	0
†W. K. Lees, c sub, b Mudassar	26
J. G. Bracewell, c Mohsin, b Sarfraz	34
E. J. Chatfield, not out	3
Extras (8 lb, 5 w, 1 nb)	14
59.1 overs. Total	250

Fall of wickets: 1-13; 2-44; 3-85; 4-102; 5-130; 6-150; 7-152; 8-187; 9-246.
Bowling: Rashid 6-1-24-0; Sarfraz 9.1-1-50-2; Qadir 12-0-53-2; Ijaz 6-1-21-0; Shahid 10-0-37-1; Mudassar 12-0-43-3; Zaheer 4-1-8-1.

Umpires: D. G. L. Evans and M. J. Kitchen

Pakistan won by 11 runs

Man of the match: IMRAN KHAN

Australians present joyful Indians with semi-final ticket

A capacity crowd, the overspill watching from the roof of the nearby multi-storey car park, and a ground lapped by sunshine welcomed Australia and India for what had become the World Cup quarter-final.

India replaced Shastri, who had made little contribution in the earlier matches, with Kirti Azad, a useful batsman and off-spinner who could well trouble Australia's abundance of left-handers. Australia had deeper problems: on a pre-match training run, Kim

Hughes's injured thigh muscle seized up and he was forced to withdraw from the side, so Hookes led Australia for the first time.

Kapil Dev won the toss and Gavaskar and Srikkanth began soundly and briskly. Lawson started with a wide, a sad portent of the plethora of extras that were to come.

The fifty came in the eleventh over when Srikkanth cover-drove Lawson for four. Thomson replaced Lawson two overs later, began with a wide, and then Srikkanth pulled him violently to mid-wicket where Border took a fine catch at the second attempt.

Lunch came at 119 for 4 in only 30 overs; the Australian over-rate was a funereal 13.3 an hour.

Kapil Dev attacked the bowling

on the resumption and runs came freely until he mis-hooked and gave a simple catch to mid-off. Six overs later, Yashpal Sharma slashed a Hogan and was caught at deepish mid-off, and an innings which constantly promised much had still failed to come to fruition.

Bits and pieces

In the context of what had been anticipated earlier in the day, 247 was a disappointing score. It had been made in bits and pieces, no one playing a major innings.

The Indian score looked more impressive when Chappell was caught low at slip in Sandhu's first over. Yallop and Wood batted with sense but in the sixteenth over, Roger Binny was introduced into the attack. He found the edge of Wood's bat and Kirmani took the catch.

Earlier, Kirmani had had problems in taking the ball which tended to keep low. There could be no doubt that Australia had the worst of the wicket, but this did not excuse their woeful batting performance.

In his second over, Binny bowled

INDIA

S. M. Gavaskar, c Chappell, b Hogg	9
K. Srikkanth, c Border, b Thomson	24
M. Amarnath, c Marsh, b Thomson	13
Yashpal Sharma, c Hogg, b Hogan	40
S. M. Patil, c Hogan, b MacLeay	30
*Kapil Dev, c Hookes, b Hogg	28
K. Azad, c Border, b Lawson	15
R. M. H. Binny, run out	21
Madan Lal, not out	12
†S. M. H. Kirmani, lbw, b Hogg	10
B. S. Sandhu, b Thomson	8
Extras (13 lb, 9 w, 15 nb)	37
55.5 overs. Total	247

Fall of wickets: 1-27; 2-54; 3-65; 4-118; 5-157; 6-174; 7-207; 8-215; 9-232.
Bowling: Lawson 10-1-40-1; Hogg 12-2-40-3; Hogan 11-1-31-1; Thomson 10.5-0-51-3; MacLeay 12-2-48-1.

AUSTRALIA

T. M. Chappell, c Madan Lal, b Sandhu	2
G. M. Wood, c Kirmani, b Binny	21
G. N. Yallop, c and b Binny	18
*D. W. Hookes, b Binny	1
A. R. Border, b Madan Lal	36
†R. W. Marsh, lbw, b Madan Lal	0
K. H. MacLeay, c Gavaskar, b Madan Lal	5
T. G. Hogan, c Srikkanth, b Binny	8
G. F. Lawson, b Sandhu	16
R. M. Hogg, not out	8
J. R. Thomson, b Madan Lal	0
Extras (5 lb, 5 w, 4 nb)	14
38.2 overs. Total	129

Fall of wickets: 1-3; 2-46; 3-48; 4-52; 5-52; 6-69; 7-78; 8-115; 9-129.
Bowling: Kapil Dev 8-2-16-0; Sandhu 10-1-26-2; Madan Lal 8.2-3-20-4; Binny 8-2-29-4; Amarnath 2-0-17-0; Azad 2-0-7-0.

Umpires: J. Birkenshaw and D. R. Shepherd.

India won by 118 runs

Man of the match: R. M. H. BINNY

Allan Border, the only Australian batsman to offer resistance to the Indian bowlers, steers the ball past Kirmani.

Bacchus and Haynes wrap it up for West Indies

Roger Binny, who tore the heart out of the Australian batting with three wickets in three overs.

Hookes with a ball of full length, and in his third, he caught and bowled Yallop off a skier. Marsh was leg-before first ball.

Border struck well, but in the last over before tea, MacLeay slashed at Madan Lal and Gavaskar at slip hung on to the stinging catch.

Eyes on the semi-final

With Australia 69 for 5 at tea, India's eyes were firmly on the semi-final. Their optimism was confirmed in the first over after the break when Hogan was taken at cover to provide Binny with his fourth wicket. The flags waved, the whistles blew, the cans were banged; India were winning.

The flags continued to wave. The large Indian contingent continued to chant until Thomson went first ball and India were in the semi-final of the World Cup for the first time.

They had outplayed the Australians and their bounding enthusiasm when they got on top was a joy to behold. Their cricket is part of their soul, and on 20th June, Chelmsford became an historic part of India. **DL**

Even without Gordon Greenidge, Michael Holding and Andy Roberts, the West Indies held far too many trump cards for Zimbabwe. Desmond Haynes and Faoud Bacchus reached their target with 14.5 overs to spare and without the slightest hint of difficulty on a placid pitch.

It was a thoroughly convincing, professional display from the two batsmen, particularly by Bacchus, who has had little opportunity to build a lengthy innings during a series that has seen the West Indies' middle order almost out of the picture since the shock opening-match defeat by India.

Paceman Joel Garner, back in the side after injury, had a useful workout and had made the initial breakthrough for the West Indies when he removed Grant Paterson and Jack Heron with successive deliveries in the fourth over with the Zimbabwe total on 17.

Zimbabwe were distinctly under the weather at 42 for 5 in the twenty-third over, but at this far from encouraging point Kevin Curran, the Lancashire League all-rounder, came in. He was eventually ninth out

The end of a disappointing competition for Andy Pycroft.

with the score on 171 in the last over of the innings, but by then had helped to add a further 129 runs and lift Zimbabwe at least some way out of the doldrums.

When Rawson was out off the last ball of the innings, Zimbabwe had pulled themselves back from the brink of total humiliation, but a score of 171 was never going to be enough. **MB**

ZIMBABWE

R. D. Brown, c Lloyd, b Marshall	14
G. A. Paterson, c Richards, b Garner	6
J. G. Heron, c Dujon, b Garner	0
A. J. Pycroft, c Dujon, b Marshall	4
†D. L. Houghton, c Lloyd, b Daniel	0
*D. A. G. Fletcher, b Richards	23
K. M. Curran, b Daniel	62
I. Butchart, c Haynes, b Richards	8
G. E. Peckover, c and b Richards	3
P. W. E. Rawson, b Daniel	19
A. J. Traicos, not out	1
Extras (4 b, 13 lb, 7 w, 7 nb)	31
60 overs. Total	**171**

Fall of wickets: 1-17; 2-17; 3-41; 4-42; 5-42; 6-79; 7-104; 8-115; 9-170.
Bowling: Marshall 12-3-19-2; Garner 7-4-13-2; Davis 8-2-13-0; Daniel 9-2-28-3; Gomes 12-2-26-0; Richards 12-1-41-3.

WEST INDIES

D. L. Haynes, not out	88
S. F. A. Bacchus, not out	80
Extras (1 lb, 3 w)	4
45.1 overs. Total (no wickets)	**172**

Did not bat: A. L. Logie, I. V. A. Richards, H. A. Gomes, *C. H. Lloyd, †P. J. Dujon, J. Garner, M. D. Marshall, W. W. Daniel, W. W. Davis.
Bowling: Rawson 12-3-38-0; Butchart 4-0-23-0; Traicos 12-2-24-0; Curran 9-0-44-0; Fletcher 8.1-0-39-0.

Umpires: H. D. Bird and D. J. Constant
West Indies won by 10 wickets
Man of the match: S. F. A. BACCHUS

Icing on the cake for England

Into the semis

Perhaps the only surprise on another golden afternoon was that adjudicator Richard Hutton should nominate the England captain, Bob Willis, as Man of the Match for his leadership. It was a point that deserved to be made, for England had reached the semi-finals before this match began and another success was icing on the cake.

Norman Cowans made his first Prudential appearance, making a good impression when he bowled downhill. Botham, angered by Press comments on his form and irritated by the rejection of a vehement appeal for a catch behind off Wettimuny, worked up a resentful pace and ended his first spell with 1981-style figures: 6-3-9-2.

Sri Lanka's last pair, Ratnayake and John, raised 33 but could not prolong the innings beyond the fifty-first over in the face of persistent England pressure.

As in the Sri Lankan innings the new ball, as bowled by de Mel, provoked a few mis-timings and mis-hits from Fowler and Tavare. The Kent captain made 19 runs in 16 overs before being caught behind, but 68 runs were on the board, and Fowler and Gower were able to stroke their way to an easy victory.

The Sri Lankan coach, Sir Garfield Sobers, admitted afterwards that his charges had not learned as quickly as he would have liked and gave England a timely reminder that, Hadlee apart, they had still to meet top-class pace-bowling in the competition. **DH**

Without doubt, the new arrangement of two rounds of group matches had been a great success. But it was all the more galling for Australia and New Zealand, who could make no excuses for coming third in their respective groups and so departing the competition.

GROUP A				
	P	W	L	Pts	Runs/over
England	6	5	1	20	4·67
Pakistan	6	3	3	12	4·01
New Zealand ...	6	3	3	12	3·93
Sri Lanka	6	1	5	4	3·75
GROUP B				
	P	W	L	Pts	Runs/over
West Indies	6	5	1	20	4·31
India	6	4	2	16	3·87
Australia	6	2	4	8	3·81
Zimbabwe	6	1	5	4	3·49

New Zealand were perhaps unlucky to go out on a difference in run-rate of .08 an over, but the real reason for their failure was the feeble effort in the second Sri Lankan game. Australia's ageing attack and thin batting line-up had simply proved inadequate.

Zimbabwe and Sri Lanka had won only one match each but went home having gained innumerable friends.

If the group matches had proved a disaster for the Antipodes, the Indian sub-continent could rejoice. India were looking ever more competent; Pakistan had managed to show their individual talents to good enough effect to scrape in.

England and West Indies had undoubtedly been the strongest sides in the early matches. But a team effort by Pakistan's stars could upset the West Indies at the Oval, while at Old Trafford, England knew that no side containing Kapil Dev could be regarded as a pushover.

On the facing page are further scenes from the group matches.

SRI LANKA

S. Wettimuny, lbw, b Botham	22
B. Kuruppu, c Gatting, b Willis	6
A. Ranatunga, c Lamb, b Botham	0
R. L. Dias, c Gould, b Cowans	7
*R. L. D. Mendis, b Allott	10
R. S. Madugalle, c Gould, b Allott	0
D. S. de Silva, c Gower, b Marks	15
†R. G. de Alwis, c Marks, b Cowans	19
A. L. F. de Mel, c Lamb, b Marks	10
R. J. Ratnayake, not out	20
V. John, c Cowans, b Allott	15
Extras (5 b, 2 lb, 3 w, 2 nb)	12
50.4 overs. Total	136

Fall of wickets: 1-25; 2-30; 3-32; 4-40; 5-43; 6-54; 7-81; 8-97; 9-103.
Bowling: Willis 9-4-9-1; Cowans 12-3-31-2; Botham 9-4-12-2; Allott 10.4-0-41-3; Gatting 4-2-13-0; Marks 6-2-18-2.

ENGLAND

G. Fowler, not out	81
C. J. Tavare, c de Alwis, b de Mel	19
D. J. Gower, not out	27
Extras (1 b, 3 lb, 3 w, 3 nb)	10
24.1 overs. Total (1 wicket)	137

Did not bat: A. J. Lamb, M. W. Gatting, I. T. Botham, †I. J. Gould, V. J. Marks, P. J. W. Allott, *R. G. D. Willis, N. G. Cowans.

Fall of wicket: 1-68.
Bowling: de Mel 10-1-33-1; Ratnayake 5-0-23-0; John 6-0-41-0; de Silva 3-0-29-0; Ranatunga 0.1-0-1-0.

Umpires: B. Leadbeater and R. Palmer
England won by 9 wickets
Man of the match: R. G. D. WILLIS

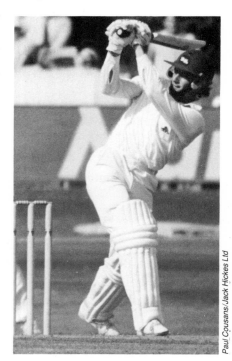

Paul Cousans/Jack Hickes Ltd

Graeme Fowler takes a six off Ratnayake during his not-out 81.

Dilley looked a much-improved bowler, but this time Qadir was not out.

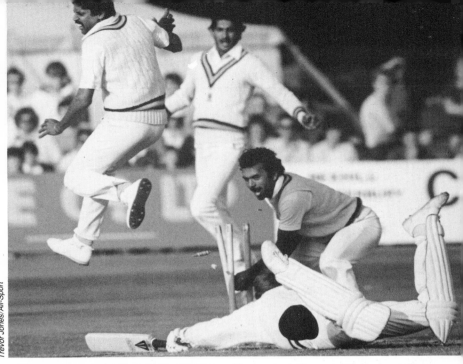

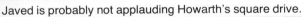

Javed is probably not applauding Howarth's square drive.

Above: Jack Heron of Zimbabwe dives – but too late.

Below: Traditional cricket grounds all round England absorbed and enjoyed the enthusiasm of supporters from the eight countries taking part.

Above: David Hookes could do without the exultant Indian supporter as he makes for the Chelmsford pavilion, another of Binny's victims.

Left: The obligatory streaker, at Old Trafford.

Shock win for Kapil Dev's men over feeble England

Above: The awesome sight of Kapil Dev in full flight.

Below: Indian jubilation as Gower falls, caught by Kirmani off Amarnath.

Mohinder Amarnath ended the 1979 World Cup with a fractured skull after being hit by New Zealand's Richard Hadlee and spent the next three years in international exile.

The only headache that could have troubled him after an all-round performance that dumped England out of the World Cup would have been caused by the gallons of champagne that flowed in the Indian dressing room after their six-wicket semi-final victory at Old Trafford.

Amarnath arrived in England in 1983 with an astonishing record of 1192 runs in 11 Tests against West Indies and Pakistan in the previous 12 months. But it was the 32-year-old's oh-so-gentle medium-pace bowling that put the skids under England, who had been hot favourites for the final.

His 2 for 27 in 12 overs was the main reason for England being shot out for 213 in exactly 60 overs. Then he followed up with 46 in a 92-run third-wicket partnership with Yashpal Sharma which set the scene for India to coast home with the comfortable margin of 32 balls to spare.

Solid launching pad

Earlier, however, when Willis won the toss and chose to bat, a large England total had looked on the cards as Graeme Fowler and Chris Tavare fluently pieced together an opening stand of 69 in just 17 overs.

With the shine off the new ball and a solid launching pad, England should have been ready to accelerate against the Indian change-bowlers. Roger Binny, however, scourge of the Australians two days earlier at Chelmsford, stepped up to dismiss both openers and suddenly England were pole-axed by nerves.

Luck was slightly on Kapil Dev's side in the vital period around lunch. He had originally intended to use both Amarnath and Kirti Azad for the fifth bowler's role, giving them six overs each.

But as the English men wilted in the midday sun the Indian duo per-

Sporting Pictures (UK) Ltd

Graeme Fowler hits out during England's brief period of dominance in the morning session.

formed so admirably that each was given a full 12-over stint and in giving away just 55 runs between them they tied England in knots.

Disappointing Botham

Amarnath claimed the dangerous David Gower, caught at the wicket playing lazily outside the off-stump in a manner more reminiscent of his early playing days, and also bowled Mike Gatting.

Azad, whose off-breaks and awkward bouncy action claimed nine English wickets in a match at Nagpur eighteen months before, bowled Ian Botham with a shooter to leave the all-rounder with a disappointing World Cup aggregate of 40 runs for 4 innings.

Sound footing

Two reckless run-outs aided India's cause and only a game ninth-wicket stand of 25 between Graham Dilley and Paul Allott took England past the 200 mark.

India's reply was given a sound footing in a partnership of 46 between former captain Sunil Gavaskar and Kris Srikkanth but when they were dismissed in successive overs, the game could have just swung back in England's favour.

Amarnath and Yashpal Sharma had different ideas, although around the tea interval they were shackled down for a spell by an accurate Allott with Botham and Marks toiling hard at the other end.

Yashpal survived a close run-out decision and an appeal for a catch to the wicket-keeper, while substitute fielder Derek Randall just failed to catch Amarnath at mid-wicket. The pair drew strongly from that good fortune. Amarnath straight-drove Allott for six and Yashpal cleared the ropes at long leg with an amazing pull drive against a Willis delivery that was fast and aimed at the foot of the middle stump.

Breathtaking Patil

Amarnath departed at 142 but by then had done enough to walk away with the Man of the Match award.

Yashpal and Patil, who contributed a breathtaking 51 not out, now guided India to within an ace of victory. Yashpal finally fell to a magnificent catch at third man by Allott when he was 61 but by then India were only nine runs short of an historic victory.

The match ended in some considerable confusion as jubilant Indian supporters amongst the capacity, sun-baked 20,000 crowd surged onto the field when Patil drove Willis to mid-off for two to level the scores.

Umpire Oslear seized a stump and prepared to defend the wicket with his life, and it took several minutes to clear the outfield. When order was restored, Willis placed all his fielders on the pavilion side of the wicket to give them an escape route against further incursions and Patil was given all the freedom in the world to crack the winning boundary and send jubilant India to Lord's for the first time in three World Cups.

GO

Part of the large, enthusiastic and noisy Indian contingent in the Old Trafford crowd.

Sporting Pictures (UK) Ltd

ENGLAND

G. Fowler, b Binny	33
C. J. Tavare, c Kirmani, b Binny	32
D. I. Gower, c Kirmani, b Amarnath	17
A. J. Lamb, run out	29
M. W. Gatting, b Amarnath	18
I. T. Botham, b Azad	6
†J. J. Gould, run out	13
V. J. Marks, b Kapil Dev	8
G. R. Dilley, not out	20
P. J. W. Allott, c Patil, b Kapil Dev	8
*R. G. D. Willis, b Kapil Dev	0
Extras (1 b, 17 lb, 7 w, 4 nb)	29
60 overs. Total	213

Fall of wickets: 1-69; 2-84; 3-107; 4-141; 5-150; 6-160; 7-175; 8-177; 9-202.
Bowling: Kapil Dev 11-1-35-3; Sandhu 8-1-36-0; Binny 12-1-43-2; Madan Lal 5-0-15-0; Azad 12-1-28-1; Amarnath 12-1-27-2.

INDIA

S. M. Gavaskar, c Gould, b Allott	25
K. Srikkanth, c Willis, b Botham	19
M. Amarnath, run out	46
Yashpal Sharma, c Allott, b Willis	61
S. M. Patil, not out	51
*Kapil Dev, not out	1
Extras (5 b, 6 lb, 1 w, 2 nb)	14
54.4 overs. Total (4 wickets)	217

Did not bat: K. Azad, R. M. H. Binny, Madan Lal, †S. M. H. Kirmani, B. S. Sandhu.
Fall of wickets: 1-46; 2-50; 3-142; 4-205.
Bowling: Willis 10.4-2-42-1; Dilley 11-0-43-0; Allott 10-3-40-1; Botham 11-4-40-1; Marks 12-1-38-0.

Umpires: D. O. Oslear and D. G. L. Evans.
India won by 6 wickets
Man of the match: M. AMARNATH

Pakistan toil as West Indies cruise in

West Indies, their confidence at a peak after five successive wins, went into the game quoted by bookmakers at 8-13 to retain the World Cup, and they underlined their favouritism with an emphatic eight-wicket success.

On another day of glorious sunshine for an 18,000 capacity crowd, Clive Lloyd's decision to send Pakistan in always looked thoroughly justified and virtually decided the outcome of a one-sided match in which Malcolm Marshall and later Viv Richards, with his third Man of the Match award in four games, played the main roles.

The pitch was pacey and the early conditions, with thin cloud and some humidity about, offered the bowlers encouragement, Joel Garner looking particularly threatening in his opening spell. He beat both Mudassar and Mohsin on a number of occasions and it was no more than he deserved when Mudassar gave him a straightforward return catch at 23 in the twelfth over.

Javed absent

Ijaz Fakih, promoted to no. 3 in the absence of key batsman Javed Miandad – suffering from influenza – produced a couple of confident hooks, but when Holding came on for the eighteenth over, he played the shot a shade too soon against his second ball and edged to wicket-keeper Dujon to make Pakistan 34 for 2.

It was hard going for the third-wicket pair with Holding and Marshall sustaining the attack started by Garner and Roberts, and it was not until Gomes came on for the twenty-fifth over that the batsmen had some respite from relentless pace.

Mohsin and Zaheer took advantage to gather runs from Gomes, but with the pair looking set to go into lunch together, Zaheer lost his wicket to a rash shot – an attempted drive to mid-wicket off Gomes – and was bowled off his pads for 30, the pair having added 54 in 12 overs.

At the break Pakistan were 88 for 3 with Mohsin on 26 and, with Gomes and Richards working through the fifth bowler's allocation afterwards, there was a chance for Imran and his partner to consolidate. They in fact added 51 in 16 overs before a lively spell from Marshall put paid to any hopes of topping 200.

Brought back for the forty-sixth

PAKISTAN

Mohsin Khan, b Roberts		70
Mudassar Nazar, c and b Garner		11
Ijaz Fakih, c Dujon, b Holding		5
Zaheer Abbas, b Gomes		30
*Imran Khan, c Dujon, b Marshall		17
Wasim Raja, lbw, b Marshall		0
Shahid Mahboob, c Richards, b Marshall		6
Sarfraz Nawaz, c Holding, b Roberts		3
Abdul Qadir, not out		10
†Wasim Bari, not out		4
Extras (6 b, 13 lb, 4 w, 5 nb)		28
60 overs. Total (8 wickets)		184

Did not bat: Rashid Khan.
Fall of wickets: 1-23; 2-34; 3-88; 4-139; 5-139; 6-159; 7-164; 8-171.
Bowling: Roberts 12-3-25-2; Garner 12-1-31-1; Marshall 12-2-28-3; Holding 12-1-25-1; Gomes 7-0-29-1; Richards 5-0-18-0.

WEST INDIES

C. G. Greenidge, lbw, b Rashid		17
D. L. Haynes, b Qadir		29
I. V. A. Richards, not out		80
H. A. Gomes, not out		50
Extras (2 b, 6 lb, 4 w)		12
48.4 overs. Total (2 wickets)		188

Did not bat: *C. H. Lloyd, S. F. A. Bacchus, †P. J. Dujon, A. M. E. Roberts, M. D. Marshall, J. Garner, M. A. Holding.
Fall of wickets: 1-34; 2-56.
Bowling: Rashid 12-2-32-1; Sarfraz 8-0-23-0; Qadir 11-1-42-1; Shahid 11-1-43-0; Wasim Raja 1-0-9-0; Zaheer 4.4-1-24-0; Mohsin 1-0-3-0.

Umpires: D. J. Constant and A. G. T. Whitehead

West Indies won by 8 wickets

Man of the match: I. V. A. RICHARDS

As an appetiser for lunch, West Indies have just seen Zaheer bowled by Gomes.

Zaheer Abbas ducks prudently under a Malcolm Marshall bouncer *(left)* but takes the opportunity *(right)* to push the score along off Gomes's more gentle off-spin.

over, Marshall, the most consistently hostile of the bowlers, struck two blows in his second over with the total 139. He had Imran, playing back and edging an outswinger to Dujon after making 17, with the second ball and three balls later trapped Wasim Raja.

Then at 159 in the fifty-first over, Shahid, having already been struck on the helmet by a lifter from Marshall, gave a gentle catch to Richards at mid-wicket. Marshall had claimed three wickets in 14 balls at a cost of three runs.

Sarfraz, caught off a skyer to mid-on off Roberts, did not last long and Mohsin, having watched the procession of partners back to the pavilion, eventually succumbed at 171 in the fifty-sixth over, bowled hitting out at Roberts. His innings of 70 occupied 237 minutes and contained just one four along with 43 singles – an illustration of his dogged application without which Pakistan would have been in far worse trouble.

The remainder of the innings mustered only 13 runs and Pakistan closed at 184 for 8 – their lowest score by 2 runs in the whole competition.

The West Indian openers, Greenidge and Haynes had little trouble accumulating 34 in 11 overs before Greenidge was leg-before to Rashid from a ball that kept low.

Buzz of interest

The arrival of Qadir at 29 for the tenth over created the usual buzz of interest and in his spell up to tea the batsmen had to treat him with

Mohsin Khan during his defiant 70.

marked respect. Haynes, however, twice lofted him for fours to mid-wicket but, immediately after hitting the second boundary in the twentieth over, was deceived by a googly and drove over the top to make West Indies 56 for 2.

After that there was never the slightest doubt that they would win in a canter. They were 72 for 2 at tea with Richards 19 and Gomes 5 and in the post-interval period, with the sun slowly setting on another perfect summer's day, they did as they pleased. Richards glided smoothly to 80, with eleven fours and a six, and Gomes to 50 (three fours) in an unfinished stand of 132 that brought victory after only 48.4 overs. West Indies had now won six out of their seven games in the competition.

The one worrying note for the cup-holders was that Lloyd strained a groin while fielding before lunch and took no further part. **RD**

Mudassar Nazar steals a quick single off the bowling of Garner.

Shock win for India means no treble for Lloyd

They came in their thousands through the still, wet streets. Long before the affluent citizens of St John's Wood had even taken in the milk-bottles from their doorsteps, knots of Indians were accosting every passing white face with the repeated request: 'Do you have a spare ticket?'

The West Indian supporters strolled along, loose-limbed, confident. They had bought their tickets long ago, never doubting that the maroon caps would grace Lord's once again, nor that Clive Lloyd would be hoisting the Prudential Cup for the third time when the last ball had been bowled.

Three Indians who had hidden overnight in the lavatories were found by tracker dogs and ejected. The security men's intercom crackled: 'They're coming over the Mound wall. Send more police, quick.' Around the ground snaked a queue of scarlet and gold ties, MCC members waiting patiently in line just like ordinary cricket-watchers until the gates opened at 9.15.

Clive Lloyd won the toss and, alert to the danger of setting the Indian stroke-makers a target on a flat pitch, invited Kapil Dev to tell his openers to pad up.

The first over was bowled by Roberts from the Nursery End, with Garner, not Holding, taking the ball next. Gavaskar and Srikkanth started with extreme caution, Gavaskar looking particularly uncomfortable.

Srikkanth cuts loose
With only two runs on the board, both scored by Gavaskar, he pushed forward to Roberts as if intending to drive, half checked and saw the ball edged firmly into Dujon's gloves. Garner bounced one at Amarnath, acclaimed by no less than Imran Khan as the world's best player of fast bowling, whilst Srikkanth, who was intent on plunder, decided that he had been respectable long enough.

He cut Garner over the slips for the first boundary; drove Roberts to the mid-wicket boundary and then, in the same over, hooked him over fine leg for six. His next boundary, off Roberts, was pure Srikkanth – going down on one knee and sweeping the ball square.

In 57 balls he scored 38 runs including a six and seven fours.

With Amarnath also beginning to open up, happiness was an Indian spectator until Marshall replaced Roberts at the Nursery End. The Barbadian, with a lower trajectory than his famous partner, often deceives batsmen in his speed and length. Srikkanth misjudged him and fell leg-before trying to hit across the line.

That was 59 for 2 in 19 overs but Amarnath assumed the role of aggressor while Yashpal Sharma played himself in and the innings continued to prosper, Amarnath taking boundaries off Marshall and then two from off-spinner Gomes when he relieved the fast bowlers.

India's disintegration began in the thirtieth over. First Amarnath lost his off stump to a superbly swift delivery from Holding that cut back. In the next over, the penultimate before lunch, Sharma drove wildly at Gomes to give substitute Logie (fielding for Haynes, who bruised a hand) a swirling catch at deep cover. At 92 for 4 off 32 overs at lunch, Indian supporters were suffering some loss of appetite.

Mohinder Amarnath, whose 26 against the West Indian pace attack in full cry helped him to win the Man of the Match award from Mike Brearley.

No. 11 batsman Sandhu takes a Marshall bouncer full on the helmet.

Kapil Dev was the remaining hope. 'Remember Tunbridge Wells' was the Indian password in the interval for the captain had taken a boundary off Richards's ritual pre-lunch bowl.

The collapse continues

He then began the afternoon by hitting Gomes for two fours and was trying for a six, over long-on, when he miscalculated and dropped the ball into Holding's hands, stationed there for that purpose. In the next over Azad turned Roberts into Gomes's hands at square leg and in the thirty-sixth over Binny did much the same, Garner having moved a little wider.

So five wickets fell in seven overs for 40 runs and long as the Indian order was, there seemed little prospect of prolonged resistance from Patil and the tail.

Another 23 were added before Patil, heaving Gomes over square leg for six, tried to treat Garner with similar contempt and paid for it with a simple catch to mid-wicket. His partner, Madan Lal, made a tidy 17 before he became another victim of Marshall's pace and at 161 for 9 with 45 overs gone this final was dying.

Then Kirmani, a good last-ditcher, and the tall Sikh, Sandhu, with no reputation to lose, faced up bravely to the fast bowling battery. Sandhu was hit on the helmet by a bouncer from Marshall, bringing reproving words from umpire Bird.

Holding, from the Nursery End, eventually ended this impertinence by summarily bowling Kirmani, India being all out for 183 in the fifty-fifth over at 3.15.

Needing only a fraction over three runs an over, the West Indies could afford to pick one ball an over so Haynes's extra-cover drive off Sandhu, for four, looked like overkill.

The Sikh, however, is deceptive. He dismissed both Haynes and Greenidge for 0 in Trinidad last winter and in the fourth over of this innings Greenidge moved across his stumps, lifted his bat to a ball pitched outside the off stump and was bowled.

The next time Sandhu dropped short, on middle stump, Richards picked him off, a low pull to the midwicket boundary as casually as a man scything daisies. Kapil Dev was then driven through mid-off and midwicket for more boundaries.

And so he continued, one four an over, until Madan Lal appeared whereupon Richards punished him with three fours in an over.

The gallop faltered when Haynes, driving a little carelessly at Madan Lal, gave extra cover an easy catch.

Emotional reception

Clive Lloyd, having hinted at his retirement as West Indies captain, arrived to an emotional reception then pulled a muscle dashing for an opening single, Haynes reappearing almost immediately as his runner.

The gallop was finally halted in the fourteenth over at 57 when the mighty Richards swung Madan Lal over mid-wicket for Kapil Dev to take a splendidly judged running catch.

Nine runs later Madan Lal came storming in again from the Nursery End to have Gomes caught at slip and, while Indians were still dis-cussing the erection of a statue to Madan Lal in Delhi, the West Indies virtually collapsed.

Lloyd, deciding counter-attack was needed, flung his huge bat at the first ball of the nineteenth over from Binny, and dropped it neatly into mid-on's hands.

The tea interval (76 for 5 off 25 overs) was no help to the champions. Sandhu, returning at the Nursery End, had Bacchus chasing a ball outside his off stump to be caught behind.

Dujon eased the pressure a little by lifting Sandhu over the ropes at square leg. Marshall, after a shaky start, settled in to remind the now jubilant Indians that he is a genuine all-rounder.

Nerves on edge

As the sun faded into a cool blue grey evening no one left their seats for long. The seventh wicket pair produced the most sensible batting of the day: the target was still little more than three runs an over. The options were running out for Kapil Dev when he recalled Amarnath, who had bowled one over previously, at the Nursery End. His first

Making the breakthrough: Madan Lal, with Desmond Haynes backing up.

Vivian Richards drives during his powerful but brief innings.

ball, a gentle loosener, was edged just as gently onto his stumps by Dujon.

That left West Indies with three wickets standing needing 65 in 18 overs. Five runs later Marshall was another to be deceived by Amarnath's innocent-looking seamers.

Kapil Dev returned immediately, bounding in from the Pavilion End, hit Roberts on the pads and won the appeal. Could even West Indies recover from such a position? Holding and Garner kept nerves on edge and harassed policemen restraining the crowd at bay for another seven runs until Amarnath won the Man of the Match award by having Holding leg-before at 140.

India were World Cup winners by 43 runs. The team were applauded into the pavilion, the clapping and cheers following them up the stairs to their dressing room.

If all India's cricketers were to choose one golden day in their short history then they must surely have voted for a victory over the world champions before the eyes of the world at Lord's.

So the third World Cup that began in shocks ended with the greatest shock of all. Perhaps the prolonged rain of a freak spring did help India's bowlers more than most; perhaps the injury to Imran Khan and the disintegration of Australia opened the way for them.

But no one can take away the fact that India beat the supposedly invincible West Indians not once but twice and then added England, the home country, for good measure.

An Indian diplomat, in the week of the final, commended an English journalist for his reference to the chivalry of India's players. 'Remember,' wrote the diplomat tartly, 'we have had 54 years to learn how to be chivalrous.'

The Indian Board of Control was founded in 1929. 25th June 1983 was their greatest day.

JAI HIND!   DH

INDIA

S. M. Gavaskar, c Dujon, b Roberts	2
K. Srikkanth, lbw, b Marshall	38
M. Amarnath, b Holding	26
Yashpal Sharma, c sub, b Gomes	11
S. M. Patil, c Gomes, b Garner	27
*Kapil Dev, c Holding, b Gomes	15
K. Azad, c Garner, b Roberts	0
R. M. H. Binny. c Garner, b Roberts	2
Madan Lal, b Marshall	17
†S. M. H. Kirmani, b Holding	14
B. S. Sandhu, not out	11
Extras (5 b, 5 lb, 9 w, 1 nb)	20
54.4 overs. Total	183

Fall of wickets: 1-2; 2-59; 3-90; 4-92; 5-110; 6-111; 7-130; 8-153; 9-161.
Bowling: Roberts 10-3-32-3; Garner 12-4-24-1; Marshall 11-1-24-2; Holding 9.4-2-26-2; Gomes 11-1-49-2; Richards 1-0-8-0.

WEST INDIES

C. G. Greenidge, b Sandhu	1
D. L. Haynes, c Binny, b Madan Lal	13
I. V. A. Richards, c Kapil Dev, b Madan Lal	33
*C. H. Lloyd, c Kapil Dev, b Binny	8
H. A. Gomes, c Gavaskar, b Madan Lal	5
S. F. A. Bacchus, c Kirmani, b Sandhu	8
†P. J. Dujon, b Amarnath	25
M. D. Marshall, c Gavaskar, b Amarnath	18
A. M. E. Roberts, lbw, b Kapil Dev	4
J. Garner, not out	5
M. A. Holding, lbw, b Amarnath	6
Extras (4 b, 10 w)	14
52 overs. Total	140

Fall of wickets: 1-5; 2-50; 3-57; 4-66; 5-66; 6-76; 7-119; 8-124; 9-126.
Bowling: Kapil Dev 11-4-21-1; Sandhu 9-1-32-2; Madan Lal 12-2-31-3; Binny 10-1-23-1; Amarnath 7-0-12-3; Azad 3-0-7-0.

Umpires: H. D. Bird and B. J. Meyer

India won by 43 runs

Man of the Match: M. AMARNATH

The greatest moment in the history of Indian cricket.

Sporting Pictures (UK) Ltd

Above: Bottoms up for Zimbabwean wicket-keeper Houghton as Gordon Greenidge sweeps.

Left: A duck for Sri Lanka's Madugalle, caught by Gould off Allott at Headingley.

The one they all wanted. Sandhu celebrates Viv Richards' wicket in the second group match – but he had scored 119.

Above: Amarnath, Yashpal Sharma and Sandhu celebrate India's epic victory over Australia.

Below: 'Don't think much of the knitting.' Umpire Oslear at the Old Trafford semi-final.

Wright of New Zealand goes to a fine catch by Sri Lanka's de Alwis off de Mel.

Leading averages and statistics

Compiled by Brian Barrett

Batting (Qualification: 4 innings)	M	I	NO	R	HS	Ave.	100s	50s
D. I. Gower (England)	7	7	2	384	130	76.80	1	1
I. V. A. Richards (West Indies)	8	7	2	367	119	73.40	1	2
G. Fowler (England)	7	7	2	360	81*	72.00	0	4
Imran Khan (Pakistan)	7	7	3	283	102*	70.75	1	2
A. J. Lamb (England)	7	6	2	278	102	69.50	1	1
H. A. Gomes (West Indies)	8	7	3	258	78	64.50	—	3
Zaheer Abbas (Pakistan)	7	7	2	313	103*	62.60	1	2
Kapil Dev (India)	8	8	3	303	175*†	60.60	1	—
J. V. Coney (New Zealand)	6	6	2	197	66*	49.25	0	2
D. A. G. Fletcher (Zimbabwe)	6	6	2	191	71*	47.75	0	2
G. N. Yallop (Australia)	6	6	2	187	66*	46.75	0	2
R. G. de Alwis (Sri Lanka)	6	6	2	167	59	41.75	0	2

Bowling (Qualification: 10 wickets)	O	M	R	W	Ave.	BB	4 wkts/ inns
R. J. Hadlee (New Zealand)	65.1	17	180	14	12.86	5-25	1
M. D. Marshall (West Indies)	70	10	175	12	14.58	3-28	0
A. L. F. de Mel (Sri Lanka)	66	13	265	17	15.59	5-32	2
Madan Lal (India)	83	8	285	17	16.76	4-20	1
R. M. H. Binny (India)	88	9	336	18	18.66	4-29	1
R. G. D. Willis (England)	73.4	19	206	11	18.73	4-42	1
V. J. Marks (England)	78	9	246	13	18.92	5-39	1
M. A. Holding (West Indies)	74.5	11	225	12	19.58	3-40	0
Kapil Dev (India)	84	13	245	12	20.41	5-43	1
A. M. E. Roberts (West Indies)	74	12	238	11	21.63	3-32	0

Fielding

P. J. Dujon (West Indies)   16 (15 ct, 1 st)
S. M. H. Kirmani (India)   14 (12 ct, 2 st)
I. J. Gould (England)   12 (11 ct, 1 st)
Wasim Bari (Pakistan)   9 (6 ct, 3 st)
R. W. Marsh (Australia)   8 (all ct)
D. L. Houghton (Zimbabwe)   7 (all ct)
Kapil Dev (India)   6
A. J. Lamb (England)   6
R. G. de Alwis (Sri Lanka)   5 (all ct)
D. L. Haynes (West Indies)   5
C. H. Lloyd (West Indies)   5

Man of the Match Awards

I. V. A. Richards (West Indies)   3
Abdul Qadir (Pakistan)   2
M. Amarnath (India)   2

Highest Individual Score

175*†   Kapil Dev (India v. Zimbabwe)

Best Bowling

7-51†   W. W. Davis (West Indies v. Australia)

Highest Totals

338-5†   Pakistan v. Sri Lanka
333-9   England v. Sri Lanka
322-6   England v. New Zealand
320-9   Australia v. India

Lowest Totals

129   Australia v. India
136   Sri Lanka v. England
140   West Indies v. India
151   Pakistan v. West Indies

Highest Partnerships

172   D. L. Haynes and S. F. A. Bacchus (1st wicket – unbroken), West Indies v. Zimbabwe
147   Zaheer Abbas and Imran Khan (4th wicket – unbroken), Pakistan v. New Zealand
144†   Imran Khan and Shahid Mahboob (6th wicket), Pakistan v. Sri Lanka
144   T. M. Chappell and K. J. Hughes (2nd wicket), Australia v. India
132   I. V. A. Richards and H. A. Gomes (3rd wicket – unbroken), West Indies v. Pakistan
126†   Kapil Dev and S. M. H. Kirmani (9th wicket – unbroken), India v. Zimbabwe

Highest Score Batting Second

288-9†   Sri Lanka v. Pakistan

Highest Match Aggregate

626†   (Pakistan v. Sri Lanka)

†Prudential World Cup Record